DONALD
WILSON

# THE PRIDE OF

# AFRICAN AMERICAN

# HISTORY

- **INVENTORS**
- **SCIENTISTS**
- **PHYSICIANS**
- **ENGINEERS**

*Featuring many outstanding African Americans and
more than 1100 African American Inventions
Verified by U. S. Patent Numbers*

## DCW PUBLISHING COMPANY

### BIRMINGHAM, MICHIGAN

ISBN: 1-4107-2874-9 (e-book)
ISBN: 1-4107-2873-0 (Paperback)

Library of Congress Control Number: 2003092255


This book is printed on acid free paper.


Printed in the United States of America
Bloomington, IN

1st Books - rev. 05/02/03

**We wish to thank everyone
*who contributed to the
publishing of this book
and continue their
outstanding commitment
to the African American
community.***

This work is dedicated to all African Americans who have managed to excel in their chosen fields and professions despite the racial discrimination and injustices they have endured. With their contributions to world civilization, these valiant men and women have formulated an everlasting legacy of role models for all present and future American generations regardless of race, creed and ethnicity.

# CONTENTS

# Foreword

In order to minimize the tedium of constantly excusing younger African American generations and blaming any lack of interest, ambition, and motivation on the obvious absence of role models of African American ancestry, let it suffice to make it clearly understood that, in fact, there is and always has been an abundance of African American role models throughout the history of the world. The real problem being the fact that these role models have simply been omitted, ignored, or deleted from our nation's history books on purpose and by design. Historically, African Americans have been significantly eliminated from history. Very little is known about their contributions with the exception of Frederick Douglass, George Washington Carver, and Rev. Martin Luther King, Jr.

Young African American males in particular have been stereotyped, labeled, mislabeled, and as a result, stigmatized. They have been the subjects of countless studies; studies that focus on the negative, studies that ultimately say the same thing because all of the information contained in these studies is based upon false assumptions. These young African Americans, especially teenaged boys, are angry, alienated, and lost. They feel they belong to nothing and nothing belongs to them. These men need to feel that they are valuable, that they can be successful, and that they can make contributions to our society. This self- worthlessness and deflated self- esteem is what happens when an entire race of people have been bastardized by denying them the history of their ancestors. What this amounts to is systematic government sanctioned racial discrimination against past and present generations of black Americans including those yet to be born.

Even today, with African Americans contributing almost $600 billion per year to the American economy, the media continues to down play their contributions. The United States has approximately 40 million African Americans (counted and uncounted). This is more people than the entire population of Canada, which is estimated at 26 million. Yet, when we entered the new century there was not one single dramatic TV show that featured an African American family on network television. The few television shows that do feature African Americans are all situation comedies. It seems the national media in this country definitely does not want anyone, including blacks, to take African Americans seriously. Canadian citizens can see themselves in dramatic family series on network television. Mexican citizens can see themselves in a dramatic family TV series on network TV, also. Even most people in third world countries can see themselves depicted in serious family TV series…but African Americans cannot. Is there any wonder that this country has no black Governors or U.S. Senators? Consequently, with the media playing such a dominant role in creating role models, where do these young African Americans turn for positive role models?..

Most Americans grow up in this country, graduating from our educational institutions learning nothing about the African Americans' participation in history. They know little about the pharaohs of Egypt, the kings and queens of Africa, the African slave trade, the Middle Passage, the African American scientist who built clocks, wrote an almanac, and helped lay out the city of Washington D.C., or the first person killed in the American Revolutionary War. They know little about the participation of blacks in all of our country's wars, the black doctor who first performed open heart surgery successfully, the black colonel who pursued Poncho Villa through Mexico but was suspiciously discharged from the U.S. Army just prior to World War I because his superiors did not want him giving orders to white subordinates, the black inventor who saved millions of lives with his traffic signal- and gas mask inventions. Many are not aware of the black doctor who developed and set up blood banks that saved millions of lives during World War II, or the doctor and chemist who developed synthetic male and female hormones which are used in treating cancer and were the precursors to the development of birth control pills. This same doctor also developed synthetic cortisone, a powerful painkiller for arthritis and a synthetic form of a drug, which meant help for millions of worldwide glaucoma sufferers. Many African Americans refused to apply for a patent because they feared repercussions. This book lists more than 1,100 African American inventions that have made this a better and safer world.

We sincerely regret that we were not able to include all of the inventions or all of the African Americans of achievement. We wanted to cover these professions to clearly show how, in spite of the adversity of extensive racism and bigotry they had to endure, they still managed to succeed. African Americans have invented and developed everything from commodes, rapid fire guns, missiles, blimps, the cell phone battery and heart pacer controls to multi-stage rockets and nuclear reactors. This book is a salute to these brave men and women who have proven to be of great courage, resourcefulness, inventiveness and creativity with the physical and mental strength to survive the insidious racism that still prevails and shadows the movements of most Americans to this very day.

Jane Y. Wilson

# Introduction

As our country enters the new century and recovers from the dreadful September 11, 2001 catastrophe, it becomes crystal clear to most Americans that we must give unlimited consideration to the true history of this great nation. Although we are constantly being berated overseas because of our country's success, if truth be known, the United States has given far more to the world than it has received. We have saved the world in two major world wars and many serious conflicts, rendered medical help and food to countries struck by natural disasters and revolutions, and provided inventions that have saved millions of lives all over the world.

It is quite reasonable to say that no class of people of modern times has made so distinct a contribution to what is popularly called "modern civilization" as have the inventors of the world, and it is equally within bounds to say that the American inventor has led all the rest in the practical utility as well as in the scientific perfection of his inventive skill. During the nineteenth and twentieth centuries the inventors of America did more than was done in all the preceding centuries to multiply the comforts, safety and minimize the burdens of domestic life. Many Americans, native and naturalized, helped promote the progress of American inventive skill and thus firmly established this country in the front rank of the enlightened nations of the world.

The time has come to address these life saving innovations and insure that the proper credit be given where the credit is due. The African Americans played a major role in establishing this nation as a world power. At the end of the Civil War, there were an estimated four million slaves and 500,000 free blacks in the United States. The slaves contributed a magnitude of human labor without which the original 13 colonies could not have evolved in a short time into a world power. At that time, four million slaves amounted to a lot of people in a country of only 31 million people. The slaves represented more than 12 percent of the country's population and the immense contribution of slavery to the country's economic growth has consistently been played down in U.S. economic histories. Most of the slave-labor force produced the country's top commodity, cotton, which became the product on which slave owners established their family's wealth. The immense market for cotton led to the establishment of the American Textile Industry in New England in the early 1800's. Other industries like tobacco, sugar and agriculture became multi-billion dollar companies because of the slave-labor that they never had to pay for, which lowered their operational costs considerably and increased each company's large profits even larger. No other segment of the American population contributed as much to this country's economic base to make it a world power than the African Americans.

The true measure of a nation's worth in this great family of nations is proportionate to that nation's contribution to the welfare and happiness of the whole and similarly, an individual is measured by the contribution he makes to the well being of the community in which he lives. If inventions therefore have played the important part here assigned to them in the gradual development of our complex national life, it becomes important to know what contribution the African American has made to the inventive skill of this country. In this instance, the African American has contributed a disproportionate amount of creativeness and resourcefulness in compiling the enclosed list of over 1100 U.S. Patents for inventions that are in daily use today in the modern world. From the corn harvester invented in 1834 to the modern day inventions of the 21st century the quality and purpose of the inventions have enhanced all of civilization.

Contrary to a misconception that still prevails, these African American's ancestors were familiar with literature and art before their contact with the western world. The forefathers of African slaves in the New World lived in a society where university life was fairly common and scholars were held with reverence. Consequently, the Africans were not without a cultural past. According to Time Magazine's Sept. 15th, 1997 issue, there are more pyramids in Nubia than in all of Egypt, and Nubia not Egypt, may have been the first true African civilization. World history clearly shows that about 730 BC Nubia rose up and conquered Egypt, establishing what became known as Egypt's 25th Dynasty. Another problem, historians now firmly believe, was racial prejudice. Many scholars didn't believe black Africa was capable of producing high civilization, so they stopped at Egypt. Therefore, at the beginning of the African slave trade with West Africa in a sad period of decline and in a midst of wreck and ruin, the new arriving and somewhat illiterate Europeans were misled by the inability of the Africans to speak English, understand the European invaders' intentions, communicate and to follow orders. With the downtrodden conditions of the continent they assumed that nothing of order and value ever existed in these countries. This mistaken impression, too often repeated, has influenced the interpretation of African history for four hundred years.

To this day, the aim of the media is, throughout the world and under the mantle of science, to make the black man believe that he has never been responsible for anything at all of worth, not even for what is to be found right in his own house and home. Many historians have tried to take Egypt out of Africa, even denying that many of the Egyptian pharaohs, kings and queens were African. In this way, it is made easy to bring about the abandonment and renunciation of all national aspirations on the part of those who are wavering and the reflexes of subordination are reinforced in those who have already prejudged based upon false propaganda.

Even when the African slave trade story is told, seldom is there mention of the fact that many times the African slaves revolted on the slave ships, attacking and disarming their European captors and actually turning the slave ships around and returning to Africa.

African and African American history has been carefully expunged from our nation's history books or distorted to such an extent the truth is not to be found. In our learning institutions today, most African American students as well as white students, go through school without ever being told about the inventions of African American inventors, scientific achievements of African American scientists or the true exploits of African American heroes. In fact in this book you will find more than 1100 African American inventions and many that the African American race has never been publicly accredited with before. In order to avoid crediting the black inventor, educational institutions refer to "the inventor of the mass produced item". Since many times the black inventor could not obtain financing for mass production, the credit would go to others who had financing available and picked up the patent rights when the 17 year term expired.

It is to these deplorable omissions that this book seeks to address in order to help restore the confidence and self-esteem of African Americans and enlighten people all over the world by displaying the prolific amount of intelligent African Americans who have contributed and are contributing to improving world civilization. There are so many inventions and accomplishments in so many different fields we sincerely regret that we couldn't include them all.

Today more than ever before, it is important for each citizen to recognize the African American's contributions throughout the history of our country. In the past their accomplishments have been shunned by racist media reporting and completely ignored by our schools' history books. In fact, our nation's history itself has been denigrated in our educational institutions and we are losing our story, forgetting who we are and how we have come this far. The American Council of Trustees and Alumni reported in 2002 that none of the nation's top 50 colleges and universities even requires history as part of the curriculum. If this is true, what happens to the history of African Americans who have helped build the infrastructure of this country? Will these valiant men and women, who have been kept a secret until now, still have to suffer in anonymity because of the lack of history classes in our educational institutions? This book offers an opportunity to help build self-esteem and self-respect to a segment of our country's society who have been denied this information due to past generations of bigotry and prejudice.

From the arrival of African slaves to North America, up to and including 2001, this book offers a review of how these people, despite the adversity of racism, still managed to excel. Although there has always been slavery throughout the world, none could compare with the ruthless African slave trade in which so many lives were destroyed. The loss of tens of millions of African slaves over the four hundred years of the slave trade, who left Africa aboard slave ships but never reached the destinations in the New World, represents the greatest holocaust of an entire race of people ever perpetrated by man against man in the history of the world. If the Atlantic should ever dry up there would be a trail of African skeletons outlining the route of the Middle Passage on the ocean floor. However, despite this horrific catastrophe of near genocide proportions, their descendants still managed to survive to lead the world in many valued accomplishments and inventions that are authenticated by United States Patent numbers. These inventions have improved the lives of all modern day civilizations and made our world a better and safer place to live.

Donald Wilson

# In 1884, France sent the United States a gift of the Statue of Liberty to honor the 200,000 African Americans who fought for their liberty in the U.S. Civil War

Typical of how the true history of African Americans has been obscured in our nation's history books is the fact that the original idea for the gigantic 151 foot statue was stimulated by the role that black soldiers and sailors played in the ending of African American bondage in the United States. The obvious intent of the French gift was in recognition of the end of slavery in the United States. The statue was created in the mind of the French historian, Edourd de Laboulaye, chairman of the French Anti-Slavery Society, who, together with sculptor Frederic Auguste Bartholdi, proposed to the French Abolitionist Society, the gift of a Statue Of Liberty to honor the 200,000 black soldiers and sailors who played a pivotal role in winning the U.S. Civil War in 1865 and this gift would be a tribute to their prowess. When the statue was presented to the U.S. Minister to France in 1884, it is said that he remonstrated that the dominant view of broken shackles would be offensive to the U.S. South, because it would be a reminder of blacks winning their freedom and the defeat of the South. However, this information remains unknown to most Americans as is the fact that the original statue had shackles symbolizing the end of slavery at her feet. Many major U.S. newspapers carried this information in the year 2000. However, the country of France will neither confirm nor deny this revelation.

# The African American Inventors

It was an extremely difficult task to research information regarding the history of the African American inventor. Unfortunately for the seeker after this particular information the public records of the United States government offer practically no assistance, since the public records distinguish only as to nations and not as to races. The Englishman and the American may instantly find out how each stands in the list of patentees, but the African American is kept in the dark. The official records of the United States Patent Office, with a single exception, give no hint whatever that of thousands of mechanical inventions for which patents are granted annually by the government, if any patent has ever been granted to an African American. The single exception was the name of Henry Blair of Maryland, to whom the public records refer as "a colored man," stating that he was granted a patent for a corn harvester in 1834 and another patent for a similar invention in 1836.

It is altogether safe to assume that this Henry Blair was a 'free person of color," as the language of those days would have phrased it; for the government seemed committed to the theory that a "slave could not take out a patent for his invention." And this dictum gave rise to some rather embarrassing situations on more occasions than one. For instance, in 1857, a Negro slave, living with his master in the state of Mississippi, perfected a valuable invention, which his master sought to have protected by a patent. Now, in law, a patent is a contract between the government and the inventor or his assignees. In this case the inventor was a slave and could not secure the patent himself. His master applied for the patent, but was refused on the ground that inasmuch as he was not the inventor and could not be the assignee of a slave, he could not properly make the required oath. The master was not satisfied with this interpretation of the law by the Commissioner of Patents, and at once appealed from the latter's decision to the Secretary of the Interior, who, in 1885, referred the case to the Attorney-General of the United States. This latter official, who was Hon. Jeremiah S. Black, of Pennsylvania, confirmed the decision of the Commissioner of Patent, and neither master nor slave was ever able to get a patent for the slave's invention. This case is reported on page 171 of volume 9, of "Opinions of Attorneys-General, United States."

Another instance of a similar character occurred a few years later, in 1862, when a slave belonging to Jefferson Davis, President of the Confederacy, invented a propeller for vessels. He constructed an excellent model of his invention, displaying remarkable mechanical skill in wood and metalworking. He was not able to get his invention patented, but the merits of his invention were commented upon approvingly by a number of influential Southern newspapers, and his propeller was finally put in use by the Confederate navy. With the barrier of slavery cast aside, a new opportunity was opened to the African American inventor, and the purpose of this book is to show what use he has made of that opportunity.

It must still be borne in mind that the records of the United States Patent Office do not show whether a patentee is an African American or a Caucasian. To ascertain what the African American has accomplished in the field of invention other sources of information had to be utilized. Finally, that the very omission from the public records of all data calculated to identify a given invention with the African American race completely destroys the possibility of arriving at any definite conclusion as to the exact number and character of African American inventions.

Judging from what has been duly authenticated as African American inventions patented by the United States, it is entirely reasonable to assume that many hundreds of valuable inventions have been patented by African American inventors for which the race will never receive due credit. This is the more unfortunate since the race now, perhaps, more than ever before, needs the help of every fact in its favor to offset the many discreditable things that the daily papers, television, and movies are all too eager to promote to further denigrate the race.

It appears that no systematic effort was ever made by the government to collect information as to the number of inventions by African Americans until January 1900, when the then Commissioner of Patents, Hon. Charles H. Duell undertook the task. Previous to that time, the United States Patent Office had received numerous requests from all parts of the country for information on that point. The uniform reply was that the official records of the Patent Office did not show whether an inventor was black or white, and the office had no way obtaining such information.

Notwithstanding this fact, however, an employee of the Patent Office had undertaken to collect a list of such patents. The list was used in selecting a small exhibit of African American inventions first, for the Cotton Centennial at New Orleans, in 1884; again for the World's Fair at Chicago, in 1893; and, lastly, for the Southern Exposition at Atlanta in 1895. It was reserved for the United States Commission to the Paris Exposition of 1900 to make the first definite effort to obtain this information. At its request the following letter by the Commissioner of Patents was addressed to hundreds of patent lawyers throughout the country, to large manufacturing establishments, to the various newspapers edited by black men, and to prominent men of the race:

**DEPARTMENT OF THE INTERIOR,**

**United States Patent Office.**

**Washington, D.C., Jan.26, 1900.**

Dear Sir:

This Office is endeavoring to obtain information concerning patents Issued to colored inventors, in accordance with the request form the United States Commission to the Paris Exposition of 1900, to be used in preparing the "Negro Exhibit."

To aid in this work, you are requested to send to this Office, in the enclosed envelope, which will not require a postage stamp, the names of any colored inventors you can furnish, together with the date of grant, title of invention, and patent number, so that a list without errors can be prepared.

You will confer a special favor by aiding in the preparation of this list by filling in the blank form below, and sending in any replies as promptly as possible. Should you be unable to furnish any data, will you kindly inform us of that fact?

Very Respectfully,

C. H. DUELL,
*Commissioner of Patents.*

| NAME. | NUMBER. | DATE. | INVENTION. |
|-------|---------|-------|------------|
|       |         |       |            |

The replies to this letter showed that the correspondents personally knew of and could identify by name, date and number more than four hundred patents granted by the United States to African American inventors. The letters also showed that nearly as many more African American inventors had completed their inventions, and had applied to patent lawyers throughout the country for assistance in obtaining patents for their inventions, but finally abandoned the effort through lack of means to prosecute their applications. The list, as of 1900, of more than 370 of the patented inventions as furnished mainly by the letters above showed that, beginning first with agricultural implements and culinary utensils, which circumscribed the character of his earlier employment, the African American inventor gradually widened the field of his inventive effort until he had well covered the whole range of patentable subjects. A study of the list disclosed the fact that the African American inventor has very often, like his white brother, caught the spirit of invention, and not being contented with a single success, has frequently by been led to exert his energies along many different lines of inventions.

Elijah McCoy, of Detroit, Mich., Headed the list with twenty-eight patents, relating particularly to lubricating appliances for engines both stationary and locomotive, but covering also a large variety of other subjects. The next was Granville T. Woods, of Cincinnati, whose inventions were confined almost exclusively to electricity and covered a very wide range of devices for the utilitarian application of this wonderful force. Mr. W. B. Purvis, of Philadelphia, came next with sixteen patents relating especially to paper bag machinery, but including a few other subjects as well. Mr. F. J. Ferrell, of New York, had ten patents on valves adapted for a variety of uses. Then came ex-Congressman Geo. W. Murray of South Carolina, with eight patents on agricultural implements. Mr. Henry Creamer had seven patents on steam traps, and more than a dozen among the number had patented as many as five different inventions.

Granville T. Woods is called the "Black Edison" because of his persistent and successful investigations into the mystery of electricity. Among his inventions may be found valuable improvements in telegraphy, important telephone instruments, and a system for telegraphing from moving trains, an electric railway, a phonograph, and an automatic cut-off for an electric circuit. One of his telephone inventions was sold to the American Bell Telephone Company, who is said to have paid Mr. Woods handsomely for his patent. Mr. Ferrell's inventions in valves laid the foundation for a large and highly successful manufacturing and commercial enterprise, which he conducted in the city of New York.

Mr. Elijah McCoy succeeded in placing his lubricators on many of the steam car and steamboat engines in the northwest and also on some of the ocean steamers, and from these he received a valuable annual royalty.

Mr. Matzeliger, of Massachusetts, is credited with being the pioneer in the art of attaching soles to shoes by machinery. Mr. Joseph Lee, of Boston, is said to have placed his kneading machine in many of the first-class bakeries and hotels in Boston and New York, from which he received a substantial royalty.

At that time, Miss Miriam E. Benjamin, of Massachusetts, was the only African American woman who had received a patent for an invention. The principle of her invention, that of a gong signal, was adopted in the United States House of Representatives in signaling for the pages to attend upon members who wanted them for errands. Formerly the pages were signaled by members clapping their hands and the noise incident to this method that was frequently a great disturbance of the House proceedings. The new system which was adopted involved merely the pressing of a button on the member's chair, which rang a small gong while displaying a signal on the back of the chair.

Another invention by a young colored man, which attracted considerable attention, was the rapid-fire gun by Mr. Eugene Burkins, of Chicago. This gun was examined by officers of the War and Navy Department, and was pronounced a valuable contribution to the scientific equipment for military and naval warfare at that time. The following description of Mr. Burkin's gun appeared in Howard's American Magazine:

"A brief description of the gun is not exactly out of place, although the Scientific American and other technical journals have long since given it to the world. It is an improvement upon all that has yet been done in the way of ordnance and the principles involved in its construction can be applied to any size of gun, from a one-inch barker to a thirty-six-inch thunderer. The model as it now stands weighs 475 pounds, measures four inches at breech, and is constructed of the finest of gun brass at a cost of $3,500. There is a magazine at the breech in which a large number of heavy shells can be held in reserve. In the action of the gun these slip down to their places and are fired at the rate of fourteen a minute, an improvement on the Maxim gun of four shots. The gun is elevated upon a revolving turret with electrical connections, enabling the gunner to direct the action of the machine with a touch of his finger. Firing, reloading and ejection of shells are all effected by electricity, and a child could conduct the work of manning the gun as easily as anyone."

These inventions show how completely in error were those who constantly asserted that the African American inventors up to 1900 had made no lasting contribution to the civilization of the age. By their inventiveness, they proved conclusively that under favorable environment he was capable of performing his whole duty in the work of mankind whether it was tilling the earth with his hoe or advancing the world by his thought, creativity, and his unlimited ability to be resourceful.

Throughout the following years thousands of African Americans have patented their inventions. The list now includes many life-saving inventions that have been contributed to world civilization and have played a dramatic role in every day living, science, and warfare and in advancing technology. This includes improvements on inventions that sanitized daily life such as the commode (toilet) that was invented by T. Elkins. Historical life-saving inventions and developments in medicine like Dr. Charles Drew's blood plasma that has been directly responsible for saving millions of lives; the heart pace-maker controls invented by Otis Boykin; and Dr. Patricia Bath's apparatus for ablating and removing cataract lenses by laserphacoprobe.

In space technology, William Harwell invented the space shuttle retrieval arm and Adolphus Samms invented the multi-stage rocket. James S. Adams invented aeroplane propelling. The resistor is one of many inventions by Otis Boykin. The torpedo discharger was invented by Henrietta Bradberry, the home security system with TV monitor was invented by Marie Brown. The motor was invented by J. Gregory, the defroster, the internal combustible engine and air conditioning units are a few of the many inventions of Frederick M. Jones. Garrett Morgan invented the gas mask and traffic control signal. J.F. Pickering invented the air ship (blimp). The revolutionary automatic gearshift was invented by R.B. Spikes. Alexander Miles invented the elevator in 1887. Rufus J. Weaver invented the stair climber wheelchair. In 1962, the helicopter, which has become an intricate part of warfare and life saving all over the world, was improved and invented by Paul W. Williams while he was employed by Lockheed Aircraft. Clarence Elder invented, designed and developed the occustat, an electronic system that automatically raises and lowers room temperatures, reducing energy demands. Meredith Gourdine invented and developed exhaust purifying systems for cars and a method to remove fog from airport runways. In 1968 Rufus Stokes received a patent for an air purification device making air easier to breathe for millions of people. Dr. Donald Cotton invented capillary liquid fuel nuclear reactors and developed a procedure using microwaves to measure how solid propellants are burned. Hermon L. Grimes received a patent in 1938 as the inventor of the Folding Wing Aircraft that was used in combat for take-off from aircraft carriers during World War II. This enabled the U.S. Navy to stock more planes on its aircraft carriers which was a huge advantage over enemy carriers. This accounted for over 75 percent of the downed enemy aircraft in the Pacific Theatre. In 1989, Lanny S. Smoot received a patent for inventing the Teleconferencing Facility with High Resolution Video Display that is used by so many major corporations. In 1971, Henry T. Sampson invented the popular cellular phone that is in almost constant use in the civilized world today.

The list of African American inventors is almost endless. Countless African Americans continue the rich heritage of their ancestors by exploiting their legacy of being resourceful with unlimited creativity which supports the fact that African Americans have contributed a disproportionate amount of inventions to save lives and improve life for all of civilization.

# AFRICAN AMERICAN INVENTORS

| Inventor | Description of Invention | Date | Patent No. |
|---|---|---|---|
| Abrams, William B. | Hame attachment | April 14, 1891 | 450,550 |
| Adams, Christopher P | Method for performing amplification of nucleic acid with two primers bound to a single solid support | June 24, 1997 | 5,641,658 |
| Adams, James S. | Propelling means for aeroplanes | Oct. 19, 1920 | 1,356,329 |
| Albert, Albert P. | Cotton picking apparatus | April 23, 1907 | 851,475 |
| Alcorn, George E. | Method for forming dense dry etched multi-level metallurgy with non-overlapped vias | Oct. 23, 1979 | 4,172,004 |
| Alcorn, George E. | Hardened photoresist master image mask process | May 6, 1980 | 4,201,800 |
| Alcorn, George E. | Dense dry etched multi-level metallurgy with non-overlapped vias | Sept. 15, 1981 | 4,289,834 |
| Alcorn, George E. | Imaging x-ray spectrometer | Sept. 18, 1984 | 4,472,728 |

| Inventor | Description of Invention | Date | Patent No. |
|---|---|---|---|
| Alcorn, George E. | Gaas Schottky barrier photo-responsive device and method of fabrication | Sept. 24, 1985 | 4,543,442 |
| Alcorn, George E. | Method of fabricating an imaging x-ray spectrometer | Oct. 21, 1986 | 4,618,380 |
| Alexander, Nathaniel | Folding chair | July 4, 1911 | 997,108 |
| Alexander, Ralph W. | Corn planter check rower | Apr. 18, 1882 | 256,610 |
| Alexander, Charles William | Self-leveling table | Nov. 1, 1898 | 613,436 |
| Allen, Floyd | Low cost telemeter for monitoring a battery and DC voltage converter power supply | Nov. 11, 1975 | 3,919,642 |
| Allen, James B. | Clothes line support | Dec. 10, 1895 | 551,105 |
| Allen, James Matthew | Remote control apparatus | June 29, 1937 | 2,085,624 |
| Allen, John H. | Pattern generator for simulating image generation | Dec. 1, 1981 | 4,303,938 |

| Inventor | Description of Invention | Date | Patent No. |
|----------|-------------------------|------|-----------|
| Allen, John S. | Package-tie | Apr. 14, 1914 | 1,093,096 |
| Allen, Robert T. | Vertical coin counting tube | Jan. 1, 1963 | 3,071,243 |
| Allen, Tanya R. | Undergarment with a pocket for releasably securing an absorbent pad | July 5, 1994 | 5,325,543 |
| Ammons, Virgie M. | Fireplace damper actuating tool | Sept. 30, 1975 | 3,908,633 |
| Ancker Johnson, Betsy | Signal generators | Nov. 22, 1966 | 3,287,659 |
| Ashbourne, Alexander P. | Process for preparing coconut for domestic use | June 1, 1875 | 163,962 |
| Ashbourne, Alexander P. | Biscuit cutters | Nov. 30, 1875 | 170,460 |
| Ashbourne, Alexander P. | Process of treating coconut | Aug. 21, 1877 | 194,287 |
| Ashbourne, Alexander P. | Refining coconut oil | July 27, 1880 | 230,518 |

# Archie Alexander was a prolific chemist and engineer who helped build the infrastructures in many parts of the country

Archie Alexander was a chemist and designer who was born in 1888 in Des Moines, Iowa. He received a BS degree in civil engineering from the University of Iowa in 1912. After becoming a designer for Marsh Engineering Co., he opened his own design firm and started to build structures all over the country. A sewage treatment plant in Grand Rapids, Michigan, the Tidal Basin Bridge and Sea Wall in Washington, D.C., the Whitehurst Freeway also in our nation's capitol. He designed an airfield in Tuskegee, Alabama. In 1947 Alexander was named Iowa State University's most distinguished alumni. In 1954, President Dwight Eisenhower named Archie Alexander Territorial Governor of the Virgin Islands, a United States Territory. Archie Alexander died in 1958.

# AFRICAN AMERICAN INVENTORS

| Inventor | Description of Invention | Date | Patent No. |
|---|---|---|---|
| Asom, Moses T. | Semiconductor devices based on optical transitions between quasibound energy levels | Jan. 31, 1995 | 5,386,126 |
| Bailey, Leonard C. | Combined truss and bandage | Sept. 25, 1883 | 285,545 |
| Bailey, Leonard C. | Folding bed | July 18, 1899 | 629,286 |
| Bailiff, Charles Orren | Shampoo head rest | Oct. 11, 1898 | 612,008 |
| Bailis, William | Ladder scaffold-supports | Aug. 5, 1879 | 218,154 |
| Baker, Bertram F. | Automatic cashier | Apr. 27,1926 | 1,582,659 |
| Baker, David | Railway signal apparatus | Feb. 25, 1913 | 1,054,267 |
| Baker, David | Signal apparatus high water indicator for bridges | Sept. 21, 1915 | 1,154,162 |
| Baker, David | Interliners to prevent tire punctures | March 8, 1927 | 1,620,054 |
| Ballow, William J. | Combined hat-rack and table | March 29, 1898 | 601,422 |

# Benjamin Banneker was an astronomer, surveyor, mathematician and inventor who helped lay out the plans for the city of Washington, D.C.

On the recommendation of Thomas Jefferson, Benjamin Banneker was appointed to serve as a member of the commission charged with laying out plans for the City of Washington, D.C. Born in Maryland in 1731, Banneker showed an early interest in mathematics, but it was under the instruction of a Quaker family named Ellicott that he was introduced to astronomy. As an astronomer he was one of the first Americans to publish an almanac. It included weather forecasts with the time the moon and sun would rise and set. Later, as a 23-year-old who had never seen a clock before, he constructed the first clock built entirely in America. He also became a writer and a teacher. Banneker's life was often cited, as proof of the African American's intellectual equality. He was a scientist whose self-taught knowledge of calculus and trigonometry enabled him to write an astronomical almanac. He died in 1806. In 1980, 250 years after he was born, the United States Postal Service issued a stamp honoring him as a great American.

## AFRICAN AMERICAN INVENTORS

| Inventor | Description of Invention | Date | Patent No. |
|---|---|---|---|
| Bankhead, Charles A. | Assembled composition printing process | July 16, 1963 | 3,097,594 |
| Banks, Charles M. | Hydraulic jack | May 13, 1930 | 1,758,640 |
| Banks, Charles M. | Jack | Sept. 2, 1930 | 1,774,693 |
| Banks, Charles M. | Release valve | Jan. 10, 1933 | 1,893,757 |
| Banneker, Benjamin | Almanac | 1792 (approx.) | N/A |
| Barnes, George A. E. | Design for sign | Aug. 9, 1898 | D 29,193 |
| Barnes, Ned E. | Sand band for wagon | June 13, 1905 | 792,109 |
| Barnes, Ned E. | Rail and tie brace | March 13, 1906 | 815,059 |
| Barnes, Ned E. | Hot box cooler and oiler | Sept. 29, 1908 | 899,939 |
| Barnes, Ned E. | Indicator or bulletin | Sept. 6, 1910 | 969,592 |

| Inventor | Description of Invention | Date | Patent No. |
|---|---|---|---|
| Barnes, Ned E. and Edmond, Berger | Automatic film mover | Jan. 12, 1915 | 1,124,879 |
| Barnes, Ned E. | Tie plate for railway | Apr. 25, 1916 | 1,180,467 |
| Barnes, Ned E. | Rail brace | Feb. 27, 1923 | 1,446,957 |
| Barnes, Ned E. | Tie plate and joint brace | Jan. 3, 1928 | 1,655,305 |
| Barnes, Ned E. | Pole, post and tree protector | June 12, 1928 | 1,673,729 |
| Barnes, Sharon J. | Process and apparatus for contactless measurement of sample temperature | Jan. 29, 1991 | 4,988,211 |
| Baron, Neville A. | Apparatus and process for recurving the cornea of an eye | July 24, 1984 | 4,461,294 |
| Barry, William | Mail-canceling machine | June 22, 1897 | 585,074 |
| Barry, William | Stacking device | June 22, 1897 | 585,017 |

# Dr. Patricia Bath's invention of an apparatus for ablating and removing cataract lenses improved the treatment of the disease worldwide

Enabling the blind to see is the greatest joy of Dr. Patricia Bath, eye surgeon, professor of ophthalmology, inventor of the Laserphaco Probe for the treatment of cataracts, and founder of the American Institute for the Prevention of Blindness. An independent thinker, she has been the trailblazer for women and African Americans in the medical profession being the first to attain many of the highest academic honors and appointments in her field. Bath completed high school in two and a half years and went on to study chemistry and physics at Hunter College in New York (BA, 1964). Her medical training was at Howard University in Washington, D.C. With her medical degree from Howard's College of Medicine she returned to New York. She was an intern at Harlem Hospital and completed a fellowship in ophthalmology at Columbia University. It was in 1981 that she first conceived of an invention that would use a laser to remove cataracts, a cloudiness that forms in the lens of an eye, causing blurry or distorted vision, and even blindness. Cataracts usually occur in people over the age of sixty, and nearly anyone who lives long enough will develop them. While her career has been marked by many "firsts" as a scientist, a woman, and an African American, she looks forward to the day when a person's work will speak for itself. During a humanitarian mission in North Africa, she restored the sight of a woman who had been blind for thirty years by implanting a keratoprosthesis. She is the holder of four U.S. Patents for her inventions.

## AFRICAN AMERICAN INVENTORS

| Inventor | Description of Invention | Date | Patent No. |
|---|---|---|---|
| Barry, William | Stacking device | June 22, 1897 | 584,842 |
| Barry William | Postmarking and canceling machine | June 22, 1897 | 585,075 |
| Barry, William | Postal machine | June 22, 1897 | 585,076 |
| Bath, Patricia E. | Apparatus for ablating and removing cataract lenses | May 17, 1988 | 4,744,360 |
| Bath, Patricia E. | Method and apparatus for removing cataract lenses | Dec.1, 1988 | 5,843,071 |
| Bath, Patricia E. | Laser apparatus for surgery of cataractous lenses | July 6, 1999 | 5,919,186 |
| Bath, Patricia E. | Pulsed ultrasound method for fragmenting and removing cataractous lenses | July 4, 2000 | 6,083,192 |
| Battle, James | Variable resistance resistor assembly | Sept. 12, 1972 | 3,691,503 |
| Bauer, James A. | Coin changer mechanism | Jan. 20, 1970 | 3,490,571 |

| Inventor | Description of Invention | Date | Patent No. |
|---|---|---|---|
| Bayless, Robert Gordon and Emrick, Donald Day | Encapsulation process and its product | Feb. 23, 1971 | 3,565,818 |
| Bayless, Robert Gordon and Emrick, Donald Day | Encapsulation process and its product | April 6, 1971 | 3,574,133 |
| Bayless, Robert Gordon | Pressure-sensitive record sheet and coating composition | April 27, 1971 | 3,576,660 |
| Bayless, Robert Gordon | Solubilization of vanadyl-hardened poly (vinyl alcohol) films useful as capsule wall material | Dec. 21, 1971 | 3,629,140 |
| Bayless, Robert Gordon | Solid microglobules containing dispersed materials | Nov. 25, 1975 | 3,922,373 |
| Bayless, Robert Gordon | Process of feeding larval marine animals | Feb. 14, 1978 | 4,073,946 |
| Bayless, Robert Gordon | Method of producing microcapsules and resulting product | Aug. 18, 1978 | 4,107,071 |
| Beard, Andrew Jackson | Rotary engine | July 5, 1892 | 478,271 |

*Donald and Jane Wilson*

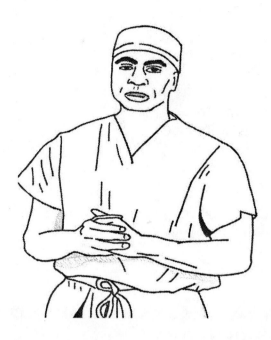

# In 1997, Dr. Keith Black moved to Cedar-Sinai Medical Center in Los Angeles where he was named Chief of Neurosurgery and began blazing new trails removing cancerous brain tumors and developing a vaccine to prevent the disease from recurring

The feats for which Dr. Black has gained international acclaim are his deft extractions of brain tumors, not just any brain tumors but the most difficult ones, often-malignant growths that are lodged at the base of the skull or in other seemingly inaccessible portions of the brain. Dr. Black is one of the few neurosurgeons in the world who specialize in brain tumor removal. He is, by most professional accounts, one of the most skillful practitioners of this highly difficult and dangerous procedure. As director of Neurosurgery at Cedars-Sinai Medical Center in Los Angeles he is helping to lead the charge against cancer on both the clinical and scientific fronts. He and his dedicated team of associates are doing clinical tests of a cancer vaccine that has proven effective in wiping out malignant tumors in laboratory rats. Born in Tuskegee, Alabama, Dr. Keith Black was the younger of the two sons of Robert and Lillian Black, who were both educators. Black is proud to be a role model for all young Americans in hopes that it may contribute to encourage and inspire them to stay in school and pursue their educational and career ambitions as they work to attain their dreams and goals.

## AFRICAN AMERICAN INVENTORS

| Inventor | Description of Invention | Date | Patent No. |
|---|---|---|---|
| Beard, Andrew Jackson | Car-coupling, (Jenny Coupler train life-saving device) | Nov. 23, 1897 | 594,059 |
| Becket, George E. | Letter box | Oct. 4, 1892 | 483,525 |
| Beckley, Charles Randolph | Folding chair | Dec. 24, 1974 | 3,856,345 |
| Becoat, Billie J. | Kit for converting a bicycle to a dual wheel driven cycle | Jan. 23, 1990 | 4,895,385 |
| Becoat, Billie J. | Kit for converting a bicycle to a dual wheel driven cycle | April 2, 1991 | 5,004,258 |
| Becoat, Billie J. | Dual wheel driven bicycle | May 26, 1992 | 5,116,070 |
| Becoat, Billie J. | Dual wheel driven bicycle | Feb. 9, 1993 | 5,184,838 |
| Belcher, Paul Eugene and Hobel, Daniel | Remote AC power control with control pulses at the zero crossing of the AC wave | May 4, 1982 | 4,328,482 |
| Bell, Landrow | Locomotive smoke stack | May 23, 1871 | 115153 |

| Inventor | Description of Invention | Date | Patent No. |
|---|---|---|---|
| Bell, Landrow | Dough kneaders | Dec. 10, 1872 | 133,823 |
| Benjamin, Alfred | Stainless steel scouring pads | June 19, 1962 | 3,039,125 |
| Benjamin, Lyde W. | Broom moistener and bridle | May 16, 1893 | 497,747 |
| Benjamin, Miriam E. | Gong and signal chairs for hotels (adapted for use by the U.S. House of Representatives) | July 17, 1888 | 386,289 |
| Benton, James W. | Lever-derrick | Oct. 2, 1900 | 658,939 |
| Berman, Bertha | Fitted bed sheet | Oct. 6, 1959 | 2,907,055 |
| Binga, M. William | Street sprinkling apparatus | July 22, 1879 | 217,843 |
| Bishop, Alfred A. | Nuclear reactor with self-orificing radial blanket | March 7, 1978 | 4,077,835 |
| Blackburn, Albert B. | Railway signal | Jan. 10, 1888 | 376,362 |

# After five years of training and work at NASA, Colonel Guy Bluford became the first African American astronaut to journey into space in 1983

Astronaut Guion (Guy) Bluford was assigned a place on the third mission of the Space Shuttle, Challenger, STS-8. This historic mission took place from August 30 to September 5, 1983. In the hours before the launch, a dramatic lightning storm brightened the night sky over the Kennedy Space Center in Florida. Guy remembers that it was dark with thunderous lightning and lots of rain, and he knew that there were an awful lot of people out there watching this spectacular event. Although many tend to think that you're thrown back in your seat at lift-off, that wasn't the case. Bluford said it was a smooth, gentle ride up. The experience of orbit was fantastic and zero-G was an especially unique experience.

## AFRICAN AMERICAN INVENTORS

| Inventor | Description of Invention | Date | Patent No. |
|---|---|---|---|
| Blackburn, Albert B. | Spring seat for chairs | April 3, 1888 | 380,420 |
| Blackburn, Albert B. | Cash Carrier | Oct. 23, 1888 | 391,577 |
| Blackburn, Charles M. | Electronic counting apparatus | Nov. 9, 1971 | 3,618,819 |
| Blair, Henry | Seed planter | Oct. 14, 1834 | 8447X |
| Blair, Henry | Cotton planter | Aug. 31, 1836 | Not numbered |
| Blanton, John W. | Hydromechanical rate damped servo system | Aug. 27, 1963 | 3,101,650 |
| Blue, Lockrum | Hand corn shelling device | May 20, 1884 | 298,937 |
| Bluford, Guion S. | Artillery ammunition training round | Feb. 13, 1951 | 2,541,025 |
| Bondu, David M. | Golf tee | Sept. 23, 1975 | 3,907,289 |
| Booker, L.F. | Rubber scraping knife | March 28, 1899 | D 30,404 |

# Otis Boykin invented an electronic device called a resistor that is used in many appliances. Boykin also invented the control unit for heart pacemakers

Otis Boykin was born in 1920 and became known as a prominently ranked electronics inventor and scientist. He began his career testing automatic control for airplanes. He developed his ability at innovation and invention in electronics with one of his first and most important inventions, a device he patented which was a small electronic element called a resistor. It is used to control the flow of electricity in appliances such as radios, televisions, washing machines and computers. Other devices that Boykin has helped develop include components for IBM computers, guided missiles, a burglarproof cash register, a chemical air filter, and a control unit for artificial heart stimulators (heart pacemaker). Boykin is also credited with developing many cost-saving devices for industry. He held over three dozen patents for his inventions and was known throughout the military and commercial world as a man of great ability. Ironically, Otis Boykin, the man who invented a device to stimulate heart action, died in Chicago of heart failure in 1982.

## AFRICAN AMERICAN INVENTORS

| Inventor | Description of Invention | Date | Patent No. |
|----------|--------------------------|------|------------|
| Booker, Peachy | Flying landing platform | Oct. 10, 1961 | 3,003,717 |
| Boone, Sarah | Ironing board | April 26, 1892 | 473,653 |
| Bowman, Henry A. | Method of making flags | Feb. 23, 1892 | 469,395 |
| Boyd, Robert N. | Dental filling composition of a coefficient of thermal expansion approximating that of natural tooth enamel | March 31, 1970 | 3,503,128 |
| Boykin, Otis F. | Wire type precision resistor (Boykin received many patents for his electronic devices). | June 16, 1959 | 2,891,227 |
| Boykin, Otis F. | Electrical resistor | Feb. 21, 1961 | 2,972,726 |
| Boykin, Otis F. | Electrical capacitor and method of making same | June 22, 1965 | 3,191,108 |
| Boykin, Otis F. | Electrical resistance element and method of making the same | Sept. 6, 1966 | 3,271,193 |
| Boykin, Otis F. | Electrical resistance element | Feb. 14, 1967 | 3,304,199 |

| Inventor | Description of Invention | Date | Patent No. |
|----------|-------------------------|------|------------|
| Boykin, Otis F. | Electrical resistance element and method of making the same | July 4, 1967 | 3,329,526 |
| Boykin, Otis F. | Method of making a thin film capacitor | Oct. 24, 1967 | 3,348,971 |
| Boykin, Otis F. | Thin film capacitor | July 23, 1968 | 3,394,290 |
| Boykin, Otis F. | Self supporting electrical resistor composed of glass, refractory materials and noble metal oxide | May 12, 1981 | 4,267,074 |
| Boykin, Otis F. | Electrical resistor and method of making the same | Nov. 29, 1983 | 4,418,009 |
| Boykin, Otis F. | Electrical resistor and method of making the same | Dec. 31, 1985 | 4,561,996 |
| Bradberry, Henrietta | Bed rack | May 25, 1943 | 2,320,027 |
| Bradberry, Henrietta | Torpedo discharge means (Bradberry invented the underwater torpedo cannon during World War II.) | Dec. 11, 1945 | 2,390,688 |

| Inventor | Description of Invention | Date | Patent No. |
|---|---|---|---|
| Briscoe, James R. | Building blocks with sides converging upwardly | April 9, 1968 | 3,376,682 |
| Brittain, Thomas H. | Level | Nov. 23, 1909 | 940,671 |
| Brooks, Charles B. | Punch | Oct. 31, 1893 | 507,672 |
| Brooks, Charles B. | Street sweeper | March 17, 1896 | 556,711 |
| Brooks, Charles B. | Dust-proof bag for street sweepers | May 12, 1896 | 560,154 |
| Brooks, James M. | Envelope moistener | April 7, 1914 | 1,092,688 |
| Brooks, John S. | Internal combustion engine spark timing control including peak combustion sensor | Nov. 13, 1984 | 4,481,925 |
| Brooks, Phil | Disposable syringe | April 9, 1974 | 3,802,434 |
| Brooks, Robert Roosevelt | Line blanking apparatus for color bar generating equipment | Aug. 1, 1967 | 3,334,178 |

# AFRICAN AMERICAN INVENTORS

| Inventor | Description of Invention | Date | Patent No. |
|---|---|---|---|
| Brooks, Robert Roosevelt | Preset sensitivity and amplication control system | June 30, 1970 | 3,518,371 |
| Brooks, Robert Roosevelt | Vertical and horizontal aperture equalization | Dec. 8, 1970 | 3,546,372 |
| Brown, Henry | Receptacle for storing and preserving papers | Nov. 2, 1886 | 352,036 |
| Brown, Fermin Charles | Self-feeding attachment for furnaces | July 2, 1929 | 1,719,258 |
| Brown, Henry T. | Combined isomerization & crack | Sept. 19, 1961 | 3,000,995 |
| Brown, Henry T. | Reactivating hydroforming catalysts | Oct. 22, 1968 | 3,407,135 |
| Brown, Lincoln F. | Bridle bit | Oct. 25, 1892 | 484,994 |
| Brown, Marie Van Brittan | Home security system utilizing television surveillance | Dec. 2, 1969 | 3,482,037 |
| Brown, Oscar E. | Horseshoe | Aug. 23, 1892 | 481,271 |
| Brown, Paul L. | Spinable stringless top | Aug. 11,1970 | 3,523,386 |

| Inventor | Description of Invention | Date | Patent No. |
|---|---|---|---|
| Browne, Hugh M. | Sewer or other trap | April 29, 1890 | 426,429 |
| Browne, Hugh M. | Damper regulator | April 28, 1908 | 886,183 |
| Bryant, Curtis L. | Protective device for automobiles | April 30, 1935 | 1,999,171 |
| Bundy, Robert F. | Signal generator | Jan. 26, 1960 | 2,922,924 |
| Burgin, Paul D. | Head lamp rim remover | Jan. 13, 1931 | 1,788,507 |
| Burkins, Eugene | Breech-loading cannon (rapid fire gun) | May 15, 1900 | 649,433 |
| Burnham, Gerald Owens | Direction coded digital stroke generator providing a plurality of symbols | Feb. 10, 1976 | 3,938,130 |
| Burr, John Albert | Lawn mower | May 9, 1899 | 624,749 |
| Burr, William F. | Switching device for railways | Oct. 31, 1899 | 636,197 |
| Burridge, Lee S. and Marshman, Newman R. | Typewriting machine | April 7, 1885 | 315,366 |

| Inventor | Description of Invention | Date | Patent No. |
|---|---|---|---|
| Burton, Gus | Emergency landing runway | June 13, 1944 | 2,351,002 |
| Burwell, Wilson | Boot or shoe | Nov. 28, 1899 | 638,043 |
| Butler, Francis Edward | Audible underwater signal | Aug. 20, 1957 | 2,803,807 |
| Butler, Francis Edward | Drill mine | Nov. 17, 1959 | 2,912,929 |
| Butler, Francis Edward | Watertight electrical connector | July 4, 1961 | 2,991,441 |
| Butler, Richard A. | Train alarm | June 15, 1897 | 584,540 |
| Butts, John W. | Luggage carrier | Oct. 10, 1899 | 634,611 |
| Byrd, Turner, Jr. | Improvement in holders for reins for harness | Feb. 6, 1872 | 123,328 |
| Byrd, Turner, Jr. | Apparatus for detaching horses from carriages | May 19, 1872 | 124,790 |
| Byrd, Turner, Jr. | Improvement in neck yokes for wagons | April 30, 1872 | 126,181 |
| Byrd, Turner, Jr. | Improvement in car couplings | Dec. 1, 1874 | 157,370 |

| Inventor | Description of Invention | Date | Patent No. |
|---|---|---|---|
| Cadet, Gardy | Acoustic analysis of gas mixtures | Feb. 28, 1995 | 5,392,635 |
| Cadet, Gardy | Process for the manufacture of devices | June 27, 1995 | 5,427,659 |
| Cadet, Gardy | Process and apparatus for generating precursor gases used in the manufacture of semiconductor devices | Dec. 12, 1995 | 5,474,659 |
| Cadet, Gardy | Acoustic analysis of gas mixtures | March 26, 1996 | 5,501,098 |
| Cadet, Gardy | Electrochemical generation of silane | April 23, 1996 | 5,510,007 |
| Cadet, Gardy | Acoustic analysis of gas mixtures | April 29, 1997 | 5,625,140 |
| Cadet, Gardy | Plasma etch end point detection process | March 2, 1999 | 5,877,407 |
| Cadet, Gardy | Acoustic analysis of gas mixtures | Sept. 7, 1999 | 5,948,967 |
| Caliver, Ambrose | Work cabinet | Jan. 5, 1926 | 1,568,498 |

# George Carruthers designed and developed the Far-Ultraviolet Camera/Spectrograph that was carried on Apollo 16 in 1972 for use on the moon

Dr. George R. Carruthers is an inventor and a visionary who has had the satisfaction of seeing a long cherished idea realized. As a child, his two great passions were astronomy and space exploration. He went on to earn a Ph.D. in aeronautical and astronautical engineering. In 1969, he invented and patented the Image Converter for detecting electromagnetic radiation especially in short wave lengths. Later, at the Naval Research Laboratory in Washington, D.C., he designed the Far-Ultraviolet Camera/Spectrograph that was carried on Apollo 16 in 1972. The device, set up on the surface of the moon, recorded distant objects and phenomena in space, feats that were impossible with cameras using visible light or based on Earth. This invention helped space exploration and played an important role in space research and advancing space technology throughout the universe.

41

# AFRICAN AMERICAN INVENTORS

| Inventor | Description of Invention | Date | Patent No. |
|---|---|---|---|
| Campbell, Peter R. | Improvement in screw presses | April 1, 1879 | 213,871 |
| Campbell, Robert Leon | Valve gear for steam engines | May 19, 1903 | 728,364 |
| Campbell, William S. | Self-setting animal trap | Aug. 30, 1881 | 246,369 |
| Cargill, Benjamin F. | Invalid cot | July 25, 1899 | 629,658 |
| Carrington, Thomas A. | Ranges | July 25, 1876 | 180,323 |
| Carruthers, George R. | Image converter for detecting electromagnetic radiation especially in short wave lengths | Nov. 11, 1969 | 3,478,216 |
| Carswell, Phillip A. | Secure cryptographic logic arrangement | Nov. 15, 1994 | 5,365,591 |
| Carter, John L. and Weiner, Maurice and Youmans, Robert J. | Distributed pulse forming network for magnetic modulator | Sept. 16, 1986 | 4,612,455 |
| Carter, William C. | Umbrella stand | Aug. 4, 1885 | 323,397 |

# In 1984, Dr. Benjamin S. Carson was named Director of Pediatric Neurosurgery at John Hopkins Hospital in Baltimore and in 1987 he became the first surgeon to successfully separate Siamese twins joined at the back of the head

Born in 1951, Dr. Benjamin S. Carson came from a poor family in Detroit. As a child, he had a difficult time in school but with the encouragement of his mother to read books instead of watching TV, he studied hard in high school and won a scholarship to Yale University where he received his bachelor's degree. He went on to study at the University of Michigan's medical school and became the first black person accepted into the residency program at John Hopkins Hospital in Baltimore. In 1984, at age 31 he was appointed the youngest doctor to the position of Director of Pediatric Neurosurgery. Dr. Carson is World famous for his skill in performing complicated surgeries on children with brain and spinal cord injuries. He first gained worldwide recognition in 1987 when he became the first surgeon ever to successfully separate Siamese twins joined at the back of the head. Both twins survived the procedure, which took five months to plan and 22 hours to perform. Dr. Benjamin S. Carson achieved his success despite growing up under privileged in the inner city and he represents a prime example and role model for having the determination and perseverance to stay in school.

## AFRICAN AMERICAN INVENTORS

| Inventor | Description of Invention | Date | Patent No. |
| --- | --- | --- | --- |
| Carver, George Washington | Cosmetic and process of producing the same (Carver refused to patent most of the hundreds of products he developed). | Jan. 6, 1925 | 1,522,176 |
| Carver, George Washington | Paint and stain and process of producing the same | June 9, 1925 | 1,541,478 |
| Carver, George Washington | Process of producing paints and stains | June 24, 1927 | 1,632,365 |
| Cassell, Oscar Robert | Bedstead extension | April 18, 1911 | 990,107 |
| Cassell, Oscar Robert | Flying machine | April 30, 1912 | 1,024,766 |
| Cassell, Oscar Robert | Angle indicator | Sept. 10, 1912 | 1,038,291 |
| Cassell, Oscar Robert | Bedstead extension | July 28, 1914 | 1,105,487 |
| Cassell, Oscar Robert | Flying machine | Feb. 14, 1922 | 1,406,344 |
| Certain, Jerry M. | Parcel carrier for bicycles | Dec. 26, 1899 | 639,708 |

# Dr. George Washington Carver developed so many products he refused to patent most of the hundreds he invented

When the scientific history of the United States is written, the name of George Washington Carver will be listed as one of this country's most productive researchers. Born in 1846, he received his freedom from slavery when the 13th Amendment to the Constitution was enacted. Most of his youth was spent in Kansas. His great interest in agriculture led him to Simpson College in Iowa where he studied botany and became known as the 'plant doctor." In 1914 bugs threatened the entire South. Cotton was still the area's main source of income and the dreaded boll weevil was threatening the crops. Carver started to teach crop rotation and diversification. Soon, farmers began to listen and sweet potatoes and soybeans were introduced into the economy of the area. At Tuskegee Institute, Dr. Carver came into international prominence. He became known as "The Wizard of Tuskegee" and he showed that hundreds of by-products could be developed from the peanut, the soybean, and the sweet potato. Bleach, shaving soap, lanolin, paper, and ink were a few of the by-products. Millions of words have been written in praise of Dr. George Washington Carver, an African American that has made numerous contributions to the United States as well as the entire world. His legacy has benefited all of mankind with new science innovations. He died in1943.

# AFRICAN AMERICAN INVENTORS

| Inventor | Description of Invention | Date | Patent No. |
| --- | --- | --- | --- |
| Chapman, Coit Timothy | Cotton planter and fertilizer | March 11, 1890 | 423,311 |
| Chapman, Gilbert B. | Integrated utility/camper shell for a pick-up truck | June 6, 1995 | 5,421,633 |
| Chappelle, Emmett W. | Light detection instrument (Chappelle had numerous patents in photobiology) | July 14, 1970 | 3,520,660 |
| Chappelle, Emmett W. | Method of detecting and counting bacteria | July 27, 1976 | 3,971,703 |
| Chappelle, Emmett W. | Rapid, quantitative determination of bacteria in water | May 24, 1983 | 4,385,113 |
| Cheetham, Margaret | Toy | April 16, 1935 | 1,998,270 |
| Cherry, Matthew A. | Velocipede | May 8, 1888 | 382,351 |
| Cherry, Matthew A. | Street car fender | Jan. 1, 1895 | 531,908 |
| Chriss, Henry T. | Footwear additive made from recycled materials | Sept. 13, 1994 | 5,346,934 |
| Christian, John B. | Grease composition for use at high temperatures and high speeds | June 30, 1970 | 3,518,189 |

| Inventor | Description of Invention | Date | Patent No. |
|---|---|---|---|
| Christian, John B. | Grease compositions of fluorocarbon polyethers thickened with polyfluorophenylene polymers | Oct. 27, 1970 | 3,536,624 |
| Christian, John B. | Fluorine-containing benzimidazoles | May 12, 1981 | 4,267,348 |
| Christian, John B. | Perfluoroalkylether substituted phenyl phosphines | June 12, 1984 | 4,454,349 |
| Christmas, Charles T. | Hand-power attachment for sewing machines | April 13, 1880 | 226,492 |
| Christmas, Charles T. | Baling press | May 25, 1880 | 228,036 |
| Christmas, Charles T. | Bale band tightener | Aug. 17, 1880 | 231,273 |
| Church, Titus S. | Carpet beating machine | July 22, 1884 | 302,237 |
| Clare, Obadian B. | Trestle | Oct. 9, 1888 | 390,753 |
| Clark, Erastus J. | Nut lock | Dec. 9, 1884 | 308,876 |

| Inventor | Description of Invention | Date | Patent No. |
|---|---|---|---|
| Clark, Samuel A. | Protective metal shield for plastic fuze radomes | July 20, 1976 | 3,971,024 |
| Coates, Robert | Overboot for horses | April 19, 1892 | 473,295 |
| Cobb, James W. | Method and system for attaching a pocket to a portion of a garment | June 20, 1972 | 3,670,675 |
| Cobbs, William N. | Locomotive headlight | Nov. 4, 1930 | 1,780,865 |
| Coles, James J. | Cap and collar case | March 23, 1926 | 1,577,632 |
| Coles, Leander M. | Mortician's table | March 26, 1974 | 3,799,534 |
| Collins, Cap B. | Portable electric light | Jan. 18, 1938 | 2,105,719 |
| Collins, Phillip A. | Bubble machine | Oct. 4, 1988 | 4,775,348 |
| Cook, George | Automatic fishing device | May 30, 1899 | 625,829 |
| Coolidge, John Sidney | Harness attachment | Nov. 13, 1888 | 392,908 |

| Inventor | Description of Invention | Date | Patent No. |
|---|---|---|---|
| Cooper, Albert R. | Shoemaker's jack | Aug. 22, 1899 | 631,519 |
| Cooper, James | Elevator safety device | April 2, 1895 | 536,605 |
| Cooper, James | Elevator safety device | Sept. 21, 1897 | 590,257 |
| Cooper, John R. | Process of reacting isocyanate and hydroxy compound in presence of tertiary amine and hydrogen peroxide | Sept. 14, 1965 | 3,206,437 |
| Cooper, John Richard | Two-stage phosgenation process for preparing aromatic isocyanates | Feb. 8, 1966 | 3,234,253 |
| Cooper, John Richard | Process for isolating a fluorine-containing polymer | Oct. 27, 1970 | 3,536,683 |
| Cooper, John Richard | Separation of distillable isocyanates from their phosgenation masses | Sept. 26 1972 | 3,694,323 |
| Cooper, Jonas | Shutter and fastening | May 1, 1883 | 276,563 |
| Cornwell, Phillip W. | Draft regulator | Oct. 2, 1888 | 390,284 |
| Cornwell, Phillip W. | Draft regulator | Feb. 7, 1893 | 491,082 |

# Dr. Donald Cotton invented a capillary liquid fuel nuclear reactor and developed a procedure to measure how solid propellants are burned

Dr. Donald Cotton is a physical chemist who was born in 1939. Nuclear chemical research was his best line of research. His hard work and brilliant mind made him recognized worldwide as an expert in his field. In his early career he worked for the United States Navy at the Indian Head Propellant Plant. He later moved to the Marine Engineering Laboratory also located in Maryland. While he was there he developed a procedure using microwaves to measure how solid propellants are burned. Dr. Cotton also invented capillary liquid fuel nuclear reactors. He realizes and understands that science is often very confusing and he has tried to break down these barriers by working as a science writer. He also finds time to consult on many major projects in Africa, South America, and Europe. Educated at Yale University where he received his master's degree and Howard University where he earned his Ph.D., Dr. Cotton spends many hours writing and lecturing throughout the world. He also plans and manages chemical research projects for the United States Department of Energy.

# AFRICAN AMERICAN INVENTORS

| Inventor | Description of Invention | Date | Patent No. |
|---|---|---|---|
| Cosby, Thomas L. | Rotary machine | July 22, 1969 | 3,456,594 |
| Cosby, Thomas L. | Closed cycle energy conversion system | July 30, 1974 | 3,826,092 |
| Cosgrove, William Francis | Automatic stop plug for gas and oil pipes | March 17, 1885 | 313,993 |
| Cotton, Donald J. | Vertical liquid electrode employed in electrocycle cells | Aug. 9, 1977 | 4,040,932 |
| Cotton, Donald J. | Capillary liquid fuel nuclear reactor | April 27, 1982 | 4,327,443 |
| Cowans, Beatrice L. | Embroidered fruit bowl wall hanging and kit | April 5, 1977 | 4,016,314 |
| Cox, Elbert L. | Presettable bistable circuits | Aug. 1, 1967 | 3,334,245 |
| Cralle, Alfred L. | Ice-cream mold and disher | Feb. 2, 1897 | 576,395 |
| Crawford, Samuel T. | Comb | June 14, 1921 | 1,381,804 |
| Creamer, Henry | Steam feed-water trap | March 17, 1885 | 313,854 |
| Creamer, Henry | Steam feed-water trap | March 8, 1887 | 358,964 |

| Inventor | Description of Invention | Date | Patent No. |
|---|---|---|---|
| Creamer, Henry | Steam trap | Jan. 17, 1888 | 376,586 |
| Creamer, Henry | Steam trap and feeder | Dec. 11, 1888 | 394,463 |
| Crenshaw, Benjamin A. | Signaling device | Dec. 15, 1931 | 1,836,705 |
| Crichton, Francis D. | Flag staff | April 26, 1932 | 1,855,824 |
| Crossley, Frank Alphonso | Titanium base alloy | July 9, 1957 | 2,798,807 |
| Crossley, Frank Alphonso | Grain refinement of beryllium with tungsten carbide and titanium diboride | Jan. 7, 1964 | 3,117,001 |
| Crossley, Frank Alphonso | Grain refinement of titanium alloys | Dec. 13, 1983 | 4,420,460 |
| Crosthwait, David Nelson, Jr. | Apparatus for returning water to boilers (Crosthwait helped design Radio City Music Hall's heating system). | Sept. 21, 1920 | 1,353,457 |
| Crosthwait, David Nelson, Jr. | Method and apparatus for setting thermostats | March 6, 1928 | 1,661,323 |

# The U.S. Dept. of Energy, Energy Research and Development Administration, and Atomic Energy Commission have called upon Dr. Ernest Coleman for his expertise as a world renown physicist

Dr. Ernest Coleman was born in Detroit, Michigan on August 31, 1943. He became a physicist and a scholar. It was at the University of Michigan that he received his bachelors, masters, and doctoral degrees in physics. After graduation Dr. Coleman served a one-year fellowship in high-energy physics in Hamburg, Germany under the sponsorship of the German government. No less than three governmental agencies, the Department of Energy, Energy Research and Development Administration, and the Atomic Energy Commission have called upon Dr. Coleman. Most of his teachings have taken place at the University of Minnesota, but it was while serving as a visiting professor at Stanford University in California that he began his most ambitious project. He developed a program tailored to help gifted but financially disadvantaged students interested in physics. This program continues today and has earned Dr. Coleman the Distinguished Service Award from the American Association of Physics Teachers. Dr. Coleman died in 1990.

## AFRICAN AMERICAN INVENTORS

| Inventor | Description of Invention | Date | Patent No. |
|---|---|---|---|
| Crosthwait, David Nelson, Jr. | Differential vacuum pump | April 22, 1930 | 1,755,430 |
| Crosthwait, David Nelson, Jr. | Steam trap | March 24, 1931 | 1,797,258 |
| Crosthwait, David Nelson, Jr. | Automatic discharge valve | Aug. 9, 1932 | 1,871,044 |
| Crosthwait, David Nelson, Jr. | Freezing temperature indicator | Aug. 30, 1932 | 1,874,911 |
| Crosthwait, David Nelson, Jr. | Refrigerating method and apparatus | Aug. 30, 1932 | 1,874,912 |
| Crosthwait, David Nelson, Jr. | Exhausting mechanism | Jan. 10, 1933 | 1,893,883 |
| Crosthwait, David Nelson, Jr. | Bucket trap | Oct. 10, 1933 | 1,930,224 |
| Crosthwait, David Nelson, Jr. | Vacuum pump | Feb. 13, 1934 | 1,946,524 |
| Crosthwait, David Nelson, Jr. | Method of steam heating from central station mains | June 19, 1934 | 1,963,735 |
| Crosthwait, David Nelson, Jr. | Refrigerating apparatus and process | Sept. 4, 1934 | 1,972,704 |

# Dr. Herman Branson's educational achievements emphasized his learning and teaching abilities as a professor, scientist and administrator

Born in Pocahontas, Virginia, Herman Branson received a BS Summa cum Laude from Virginia State College in 1936. In 1939 he received his Ph.D. in physics from the University of Cincinnati. Branson was appointed Assistant Professor of physics and chemistry at Howard University, 1941-1943 and was named Director of Experimental Science and Mathematics W Technology Program in physics at Howard. In 1947, Dr. Branson was named Director of the Office of Naval Research and Atomic Energy Commission Projects in Physics at Howard University. From 1946 to 1950 he was named Director of the Research Corporation Project at Howard University. In 1944, Dr. Branson became a full professor of physics and was made Chairman of the Physics Department of Howard University from 1941 to 1968. From 1968 to 1970, Dr. Herman Branson was selected as President of Central State University. In 1970, Dr. Herman Branson became the President of Lincoln University and served until his retirement in 1985. Dr. Branson's research interests were in mathematical biology and protein structure. He was a member of many honor societies. Dr. Herman Branson died in 1995.

# AFRICAN AMERICAN INVENTORS

| Inventor | Description of Invention | Date | Patent No. |
| --- | --- | --- | --- |
| Crosthwait, David Nelson, Jr. | Refrigerating method and apparatus | Sept. 4, 1934 | 1,972,705 |
| Crosthwait, David Nelson, Jr. | Steam heating system | Oct. 16, 1934 | 1,977,303 |
| Crosthwait, David Nelson, Jr. | Steam heating apparatus | Oct. 16, 1934 | 1,977,304 |
| Crosthwait, David Nelson, Jr. | Vacuum heating system | Jan. 1, 1935 | 1,986,391 |
| Crosthwait, David Nelson, Jr. | Remote control proportional movement motor | July 9, 1935 | 2,007,240 |
| Crosthwait, David Nelson, Jr. | Method of heating | Dec. 15, 1936 | 2,064,197 |
| Crosthwait, David Nelson, Jr. | Effective temperature thermostat | July 6, 1937 | 2,086,258 |
| Crosthwait, David Nelson, Jr. | Effective temperature control | Oct. 5, 1937 | 2,094,738 |
| Crosthwait, David Nelson, Jr. | Exhausting method and apparatus | Oct. 19, 1937 | 2,096,226 |
| Crosthwait, David Nelson, Jr. | One pipe heating system regulating plate | Dec. 14, 1937 | 2,102,197 |

# David Crosthwait was granted 114 patents by countries throughout the world as he designed systems that are vital to heating, cooling, ventilation and air conditioning

David Crosthwait was an engineering technologist who was born in Nashville, Tenn. in 1898. He designed the systems that control the heating and ventilation facilities in the huge Rockefeller Center Complex in New York City. In 1913, Crosthwait received a bachelor's degree in mechanical engineering. Sixty-two years later his alma mater, Purdue University in Indiana, granted him an honorary Ph.D. in the same field. He was cited for his many accomplishments, including 114 patents granted by countries throughout the world. He received 34 patents from the United States and 80 patents from foreign countries. During the course of his career, he designed systems that are vital to the heating and cooling industry. He made major contributions to the technologies of refrigeration, heating, cooling, ventilation, and air conditioning. For most of his professional life he worked for the Dunham Company of Chicago, heading their Marshall, Iowa Research Facility. After his active retirement he spent the last years of his life as a professor at Purdue University. Crosthwait died in 1976.

## AFRICAN AMERICAN INVENTORS

| Inventor | Description of Invention | Date | Patent No. |
|---|---|---|---|
| Crosthwait, David Nelson, Jr. | Regulating radiator valve | April 12, 1938 | 2,114,139 |
| Crumble, James H. | Float operated mechanism | Sept. 11, 1945 | 2,384,536 |
| Curtis, William Childs | Airborne moving-target indicating system | July 5, 1977 | 4,034,373 |
| Dacons, Joseph Carl | Process for the manufacturing of nitroform and its salts | March 17, 1964 | 3,125,606 |
| Dacons, Joseph Carl | Dodecanitroquater-phenyl | June 17, 1969 | 3,450,778 |
| Dacons, Joseph Carl | Recrystallization of hexanitrostilbene from nitric acid and water | April 7, 1981 | 4,260,847 |
| Dammond, William H. | Safety system for operating railroads | June 19, 1906 | 823,513 |
| Darkins, John Thomas | Ventilator | Feb. 19, 1895 | 534,322 |
| Davidson, Shelby J. | Paper-rewind mechanism for adding machines | April 14, 1908 | 884,721 |
| Davis, Israel D. | Tonic | Nov. 2, 1886 | 351,829 |

# Dr. Ulysses Grant Daily was a renown physician and worldwide medical correspondent

Dr. Ulysses Grant Daily was born in 1885 and he had an astonishing career in medicine. Shortly after his graduation from medical school he was appointed an instructor of anatomy at Northwestern University. He was also surgical assistant to the great Dr. Daniel Hale Williams, editor of the Journal of the National Medical Association, and one of the founding members of the International College of Surgeons. It was while working with Dr. Williams at Chicago's Provident Hospital that Dr. Daily first came to the attention of several prominent European physicians. He spent several years practicing in London, Paris, and Vienna. In 1926 he established his own hospital and sanitarium. His reputation was so worldwide that he served as medical correspondent for newspapers as far away as Pakistan. He traveled extensively for the International College of Surgeons and the United States State Department. He was named Honorary Counsel to Haiti in 1954. Dr. Daily died in 1961.

## AFRICAN AMERICAN INVENTORS

| Inventor | Description of Invention | Date | Patent No. |
|---|---|---|---|
| Davis, Stephen H. | Load weighing and totaling device for cranes, hoists and the like | July 20, 1943 | 2,324,769 |
| Davis, Stephen S. | Flexible walled wind tunnel nozzle | April 26, 1960 | 2,933,922 |
| Davis, William D. | Riding saddle | Oct. 6, 1896 | 568,939 |
| Davis, William R., Jr. | Library table | Sept. 24, 1878 | 208,378 |
| Davis, William R., Jr. | Game table | May 10, 1887 | 362,611 |
| Dean, Mark E. | Microcomputer system with bus control means for peripheral processing devices | July 9, 1985 | 4,528,626 |
| Dedmon, Robert | Combined sleigh and boat | June 4, 1929 | 1,716,230 |
| Deitz, William A. | Shoe | April 30, 1867 | 64,205 |
| Delaotch, Essex | Motor control system for self-serving tables | Sept. 4, 1923 | 1,466,890 |

# In 1940, Dr. Charles Drew developed blood plasma, the first blood bank and saved countless lives

Charles Richard Drew was born in 1904 in Washington, D.C. He graduated from Amherst College in Massachusetts in 1926 and received his medical degree from McGill Medical College in Montreal in 1933. As an intern at Montreal General Hospital he pioneered in blood research. In 1940 he published "Banked Blood: A Study in Blood Preservation." At the request of Dr. John Beattie of Britain's Royal College of Surgeons, Drew started the "Blood For Britain" project which consisted of collecting and drying blood plasma to be used for transfusion on the battlefield. His success abroad led to Drew being awarded an honorary D.Sc. degree from Columbia University. He served as the Director of the American Red Cross Blood Bank in 1941 and later as chief surgeon of Freedmen's Hospital in Washington, D.C. Drew continually disputed any scientific basis indicating blood differences according to race. The government planned a national blood-collection program for its armed forces in 1941, which Drew was asked to help establish. But on orders from the military, black donors were barred; only "white" blood was deemed acceptable, which led to the absurdity that Drew himself was prohibited from donating blood in the program he headed. At some point, the policy changed to the extent that African Americans could donate blood, but "black" blood was segregated for use by black servicemen only. Drew finally resigned from the program in disgust and in 1946 he became Medical Director of Freedmen's Hospital. In April 1950, he died from an auto accident in North Carolina because the hospital he was taken to lacked any blood plasma that might have saved his life.

## AFRICAN AMERICAN INVENTORS

| Inventor | Description of Invention | Date | Patent No. |
|---|---|---|---|
| Demon, Ronald S. | Shoe sole with an adjustable support pattern | Sept. 29, 1998 | 5,813,142 |
| Dent, Anthony L. | Rehydrated silica gel dentifrice abrasive | Aug. 24, 1982 | 4,346,071 |
| Dent, Anthony L. | Toothpaste containing ph- adjusted zeolite | Sept. 14, 1982 | 4,349,533 |
| Dent, Benjamin A. | Procedure entry for a data processor employing a stack | Dec. 15, 1976 | 3,548,384 |
| Dickenson, Robert C. | Trolley guard | Aug. 26, 1970 | 1,314,130 |
| Dickinson, Joseph Hunter | Reed-Organ | May 2, 1899 | 624,192 |
| Dickinson, Joseph Hunter | Adjustable tracker for pneumatic playing attachments | March 23, 1909 | 915,942 |
| Dickinson, Joseph Hunter | Volume-controlling means for mechanical musical instruments | June 29, 1909 | 926,178 |
| Dickinson, Joseph Hunter | Player-piano | June 11, 1912 | 1,028,996 |

| Inventor | Description of Invention | Date | Patent No. |
|---|---|---|---|
| Dickinson, Joseph Hunter | Phonograph | Jan. 18, 1918 | 1,252,411 |
| Diuguid, Lincoln Isaiah | Burning efficiency enhancement method | Sept. 3, 1985 | 4,539,015 |
| Dixon, James | Car-coupling | March 29, 1892 | 471,843 |
| Dixon, Samuel, Jr. and Malik, Roger J. | Monolithic doped barrier subharmonic mixer | Jan. 7, 1986 | 4,563,773 |
| Dixon, Samuel, Jr., AuCoin, Thomas R. and Malik, Roger J. | Monolithic planar doped barrier limiter | March 31, 1987 | 4,654,609 |
| Dorcas, Lewis B. | Stove | Oct. 15, 1907 | 868,417 |
| Dorman, Linneaus Cuthbert | 3,5-Dihalo-4-cyanoalkoxy phenols (Dorman was a prolific inventor with many chemical patents). | Sept. 23, 1969 | 3,468,926 |
| Dorman, Linneaus Cuthbert | Absorbents for airborne formaldehyde | May 14, 1985 | 4,517,111 |

# In 1889, Frederick Douglass, an African American leader, was appointed U.S. Minister to Haiti

Frederick Douglass was born a slave in February 1817 in Tuckahoe, Maryland, with the name of Frederick Augustus Washington Bailey. After 20 years in slavery he fled to New Bedford, Massachusetts, by disguising himself as a sailor. In New York City, on his way to New Bedford, he took the name Douglass. In his first ten years of freedom Douglass lived in Massachusetts, where for three years he lived a hand-to-mouth existence. When he learned of a slavery abolition society made up of Negroes, he joined their ranks, leaving only to become a full-time agent of the Massachusetts, Anti-Slavery Society. He was greatly impressed when, during one meeting at the Anti-Slavery Society he met William Lloyd Garrison, a white journalist, reformer and noted abolitionist who wrote his first anti-slavery article in 1828. Douglass' Association with Garrison and Wendell Phillips along with their fellow reformers, encouraged Douglass to launch his own abolitionist newspaper in 1847, The North Star, which he published for 16 years. In 1848 he took a prominent part in the Seneca Falls Convention in New York which formally inaugurated the Woman's Rights Movement in the United States. During the Civil War Douglass recruited black troops for the Union Army and he urged the Lincoln Administration to work forcefully against slavery. Beginning in 1877 he received high federal appointments from three successive presidents, which included Marshall of the District of Columbia, Recorder of Deeds for the District, and U.S. Minister to the Republic of Haiti. Frederick Douglass was respected by world leaders when he died at his home in 1895.

# AFRICAN AMERICAN INVENTORS

| Inventor | Description of Invention | Date | Patent No. |
|---|---|---|---|
| Dorman, Linneaus Cuthbert | Composites of unsintered calcium phosphates and synthetic biodegradable polymers useful as hard tissue prosthetics | June 27, 1989 | 4,842,604 |
| Dorsey, Osbourn | Door-holding device | Dec. 10, 1878 | 210,764 |
| Dorticus, Clatonia Joaquin | Device for applying coloring liquids to sides of soles or heels of shoes | March 19, 1895 | 535,820 |
| Dorticus, Clatonia Joaquin | Machine for embossing photographs | April 16, 1895 | 537,442 |
| Dorticus, Clatonia Joaquin | Photographic print washer | April 23, 1895 | 537,968 |
| Dorticus, Clatonia Joaquin | Hose leak stop | July 18, 1899 | 629,315 |
| Douglass, William | Self-binding harvester | May 2, 1905 | 789,010 |
| Douglass, William | Band-twister | May 2, 1905 | 789,120 |
| Douglass, William | Carrier chain | May 2, 1905 | 789,122 |

| Inventor | Description of Invention | Date | Patent No. |
|---|---|---|---|
| Downing, Gertrude E. and Desjardin, William P. | Reciprocating corner and baseboard cleaning auxiliary attachment for rotary floor treatment machines | Feb. 13, 1973 | 3,715,772 |
| Downing, Philip B. | Street railway switch | June 17, 1890 | 430,118 |
| Downing, Philip B. | Street letter box | Oct. 27, 1891 | 462,092 |
| Downing, Philip B. | Letter box | Oct. 27, 1891 | 462,093 |
| Doyle, James | Serving apparatus for dining rooms | Oct. 2, 1900 | 659,057 |
| Doyle, James | Automatic serving system | March 5, 1912 | 1,019,137 |
| Doyle, James | Server for automatic serving systems | June 2, 1914 | 1,098,788 |
| Dugger, Cortland Otis | Method for growing single oxide crystals | July 27, 1971 | 3,595,803 |
| Dugger, Cortland Otis | Solid state laser produced by a chemical reaction between a germinate and an oxide dopant | Nov. 30, 1971 | 3,624,547 |

# Annie Easley's professional expertise as an aeronautics researcher and computer scientist made her a vital part of NASA

Annie Easley was an aeronautics researcher who was born on April 23, 1933. She joined thousands of people who were working on ways to conserve precious energy. Easley specialized in the design of computer programs for energy conservation. A native of Birmingham, Alabama, she received her degree in mathematics from Cleveland State University. Shortly after that she went to work for NASA (National Aeronautics and Space Administration), Lewis Research Center and its predecessor agency NACA. She has been a part of the NASA research team ever since. Some of the projects that she has been involved with include a study of the life of batteries for electric cars, a study on the most efficient forms of energy conservation and ways that wind and solar power can be better utilized. Easley developed and implemented the computer code used in determining solar, wind and energy research projects for NASA. Annie Easley is one of a growing number of women who are making major contributions to the world of energy research and development.

# AFRICAN AMERICAN INVENTORS

| Inventor | Description of Invention | Date | Patent No. |
|---|---|---|---|
| Dugger, Cortland Otis | Aluminum nitride single crystal growth from a molten mixture with calcium nitride | Jan. 20, 1976 | 3,933,573 |
| Dunnington, James Henry | Horse detacher | March 16,1897 | 578,979 |
| Dyer, Charles A. | Teaching aid | May 15, 1973 | 3,732,632 |
| Edelin, Benedict F. | Pneumatic toy pistol | Jan. 9, 1923 | 1,441,975 |
| Edmonds, Thomas Henry | Separating screen | July 20, 1897 | 586,724 |
| Elder, Clarence L. | Timing device | Jan. 12, 1965 | 3,165,188 |
| Elder, Clarence L. | Non-capsizable container | Feb. 6, 1968 | 3,367,525 |
| Elder, Clarence L. | Sweepstake programmer | Jan. 19, 1971 | 3,556,531 |
| Elder, Clarence L. | Programmed association game | July 20, 1971 | 3,594,003 |
| Elder, Clarence L. | Random unit generator amusement device | Nov. 6, 1973 | 3,770,269 |

## Clarence Elder invented the Occustat System that connects a room to an electronic beam that raises and lowers room temperatures to conserve energy

Clarence L. Elder is an electronics inventor who was born in 1935. An occustat is a fascinating bit of machinery that helps to save vast amounts of energy and was invented, designed and developed by Elder. This system connects rooms to an electronic beam. There is then an attachment made to the building entrance to monitor the number of people passing in or out of the room and the light beam is activated raising and lowering the temperature according to the number of people inside the room. This device reduces energy demand and achieves energy savings of up to thirty percent. Elder is a native of Georgia who earned his degree at Morgan State College. He is also head of his own research and design company. Elder has been awarded 12 U.S. and foreign patents, trademarks, and copyrights. In 1969, Elder was honored by the New York International Patent Exposition for outstanding achievement in the field of electronics and his contributions in energy conservation.

## AFRICAN AMERICAN INVENTORS

| Inventor | Description of Invention | Date | Patent No. |
|---|---|---|---|
| Elder, Clarence L. | Bidirectional monitoring and control system | Dec. 28, 1976 | 4,000,400 |
| Elkins, Thomas | Combined dining, ironing table, and quilting frame | Feb. 22, 1870 | 100,020 |
| Elkins, Thomas | Chamber commode | Jan. 9, 1872 | 122,518 |
| Elkins, Thomas | Refrigerating apparatus | Nov. 4, 1879 | 221,222 |
| Emile, Philip E. | Transistorized gating circuit | May 2, 1961 | 2,982,868 |
| Emile, Philip E. | Transistorized multivibrator circuit adapted to oscillate for only a predetermined time | Oct. 24, 1961 | 3,005,963 |
| Engram, Robert L. | Shock falsing inhibitor circuit for a plural tone receiver | April 23, 1974 | 3,806,938 |
| Evans, James C. | Airplane appliance | March 11, 1930 | 1,749,858 |
| Evans, John H. | Convertible settee and bed | Oct. 5, 1897 | 591,095 |
| Faulkner, Henry | Ventilated shoe | April 29, 1890 | 426,495 |

| Inventor | Description of Invention | Date | Patent No. |
|---|---|---|---|
| Ferrell, Frank J. | Steam trap | Feb. 11, 1890 | 420,993 |
| Ferrell, Frank J. | Apparatus for melting snow | May 27,1890 | 428,670 |
| Ferrell, Frank J. | Valve | May 27, 1890 | 428,671 |
| Ferrell, Frank J. | Valve | April 14, 1891 | 450,451 |
| Ferrell, Frank J. | Valve | Nov. 10, 1891 | 462,762 |
| Ferrell, Frank J. | Valve | Jan. 26, 1892 | 467,796 |
| Fisher, David A. | Joiners – clamp | April 20, 1875 | 162,281 |
| Fisher, David A. | Furniture casters | March 14, 1876 | 174,794 |
| Flemmings, Robert F., Jr. | Guitar | March 30, 1886 | 338,727 |
| Fletcher, Sylvester J. | Refuse container | Sept. 18, 1990 | D310,744 |

# In 1993, the outspoken Dr. Joycelyn Elders survived a senate confirmation battle to become the nation's first African American U.S. Surgeon General

Born Minnie Lee Jones in Schaal, Arkansas, the eldest of eight children, she was raised in a three-room cabin without plumbing or electricity and never saw a doctor until she was grown. She proudly will detail to anyone her parents' struggle to buy and keep their own farm, and her mother's insistence that she become somebody important. After graduating from high school at age 15 as valedictorian, she won a full scholarship to Philander Smith College in Arkansas, served in the U. S. Army as a lieutenant, and received her medical degree from the University of Arkansas Medical School on the GI Bill. She joined its faculty as a pediatric endocrinologist in 1967. Along the way she changed her name to Joycelyn, married a high school basketball coach, Oliver Elders, and had two sons. In 1987, Governor Bill Clinton made her Director of Arkansas Department of Public Health and later, as U.S. President, he appointed her U.S. Surgeon General. The end came in December 1994. Elders' positions on several passionate subjects added more controversy to an administration already heavily overburdened with controversy on abortion, sex, and drugs and her resignation was reluctantly requested and submitted.

## AFRICAN AMERICAN INVENTORS

| Inventor | Description of Invention | Date | Patent No. |
|---|---|---|---|
| Forbes, Dennis A. | Design for a card for a chemistry card game | April 17, 1934 | D91,996 |
| Francis, Dawn E. | Novel organic fertilizer and production thereof | Sept. 18, 1990 | 4,957,534 |
| Freeman, Louis W. | Cuff for trousers | May 19, 1931 | 1,805,577 |
| Frye, Clara C. | Surgical appliance | March 19, 1907 | 847,758 |
| Frye, Irvin S. | Adjustable shackle | Sept. 23, 1969 | 3,468,123 |
| Gant, Virgil Arnett | Method for treating hair | June 23, 1953 | 2,643,375 |
| Gant, Virgil Arnett | Hair treating composition and method of use for setting | June 19, 1956 | 2,750,947 |
| Gant, Virgil Arnett | Ammonium polysiloxanolate hair treating composition and method for using same | April 2, 1957 | 2,787,274 |
| Garner, Albert Y. | Novel phosphonyl polymers | March 31, 1964 | 3,127,357 |

| Inventor | Description of Invention | Date | Patent No. |
|----------|-------------------------|------|------------|
| Garner, Albert Y. | Flame retardant | Nov. 2, 1976 | 3,989,702 |
| Gaskins, Frances C. | Sun protectant composition and method | Feb. 21, 1989 | 4,806,344 |
| Gay, Eddie Charles | Cathode for a secondary electrochemical cell | Sept. 23, 1975 | 3,907,589 |
| Gay, Eddie Charles | Method of preparing electrodes with porous current collector structures and solid reactants for secondary electrochemical cells | Jan. 20, 1976 | 3,933,520 |
| Gay, Eddie Charles | Compartmented electrode structure | June 14, 1977 | 4,029,860 |
| Gill, Vincent A. | Quick disconnect valved coupling | Aug. 9, 1960 | 2,948,553 |
| Gilliard, Joseph W. | Car park | Nov. 20, 1956 | 2,771,200 |
| Gloster, Clay S. | Method and apparatus for high precision weighted random pattern generation | Aug. 27, 1991 | 5,043,988 |

# Philip Emeagwali uses his mathematical and computer expertise to develop methods for extracting more petroleum from oil fields

Philip Emeagwali is a computer scientist who uses his mathematical and computer expertise to develop methods for extracting more petroleum from oil fields. It was his formula that used 65,000 separate computer processors to perform 3.1 billion calculations per second in 1989. That astounding feat led to computer scientists comprehending the capabilities of supercomputers and the practical applications of creating a system that allowed multiple computers to communicate. He is recognized as one of *the fathers of the Internet.* Supercomputers range in price from $30 million to $100 million, and computer companies had reservations about building them for difficulties in programming and fear few agencies would make such high cost purchases. Future applications for Emeagwali's breakthroughs with the use of data generated by massively parallel computers include weather forecasting and the study of global warming. He also successfully programmed the supercomputers.

## AFRICAN AMERICAN INVENTORS

| Inventor | Description of Invention | Date | Patent No. |
|---|---|---|---|
| Goldsberry, Ronald E. | Ultraviolet and thermally stable polymer compositions | June 22, 1976 | 3,965,096 |
| Goode, Sarah H. | Cabinet bed | July 14, 1885 | 322,177 |
| Gourdine, Meredith C. | Electrogasdynamic method and apparatus for detecting the properties of particular matter entrained in gases | June 10, 1969 | 3,449,667 |
| Gourdine, Meredith C. | Improved acoustic image reproduction system using a piezoelectric printer and electrogasdynamics | April 6, 1971 | 3,573,845 |
| Gourdine, Meredith C. | Turbulence inducing electrogasdynamic precipitator | June 1, 1971 | 3,581,468 |
| Gourdine, Meredith C. | Electrogasdynamic systems and methods | June 1, 1971 | 3,582,694 |
| Gourdine, Meredith C. | Alternating current systems employing multiple electrogasdynamic devices | June 15, 1971 | 3,585,420 |

# Meredith Gourdine is a prolific inventor who developed exhaust purifying systems for cars and invented ways to remove fog from runways

Meredith Gourdine is a prolific inventor, pioneering engineer, businessman, medal winning athlete, and all-around role model for young and old African Americans. In 1962, he became chief scientist of the Curtis Wright Corporation's Aero Division. In 1964, he launched his own research and development company, Gourdine Systems. This company has developed exhaust-purifying systems for cars; ways to reduce smoke pollution from old, incinerator-type furnaces, and a way to remove fog from airport runways. Despite the dark glasses he wears that hide his sightless eyes, Gourdine displays the cool and confident appearance of a man of limitless vision who continues to contribute to world civilization.

## AFRICAN AMERICAN INVENTORS

| Inventor | Description of Invention | Date | Patent No. |
| --- | --- | --- | --- |
| Gourdine, Meredith C. | Copying system using electrogasdynamics | July 13, 1971 | 3,592,541 |
| Gourdine, Meredith C. | Electrogasdynamic converter with resistive channel | Oct. 12, 1971 | 3,612,923 |
| Gourdine, Meredith C. | Electrostatic painting method and apparatus | Oct. 19, 1971 | 3,613,993 |
| Gourdine, Meredith C. | Electrogasdynamic precipitator utilizing retarding fields | March 21, 1972 | 3,650,092 |
| Gourdine, Meredith C. | Method and apparatus for electrogasdynamic coating | June 27, 1972 | 3,673,463 |
| Gourdine, Meredith C. | Electrostatic precipitator system | Dec. 5, 1972 | 3,704,572 |
| Gourdine, Meredith C. | Electrostatic mass per unit volume dust monitor | Feb. 27, 1973 | 3,718,029 |
| Gourdine, Meredith C. | Apparatus for suppressing airborne particles | Sept. 11, 1973 | 3,757,491 |
| Gourdine, Meredith C. | Electrogasdynamic coating system | Feb. 21, 1984 | 4,433,003 |

| Inventor | Description of Invention | Date | Patent No. |
|---|---|---|---|
| Gourdine, Meredith C. | Electrogasdynamic coating system | Feb. 12, 1985 | 4,498,631 |
| Gourdine, Meredith C. | Method and apparatus for improved cooling of hot metals | Dec. 3, 1985 | 4,555,909 |
| Gourdine, Meredith C. | Electrogasdynamic coating system | March 4, 1986 | 4,574,092 |
| Gourdine, Meredith C. | Method for airport fog precipitation | June 9, 1987 | 4,671,805 |
| Gourdine, Meredith C. | Method and apparatus for producing multi-vortex fluid flow | July 25, 1989 | 4,850,537 |
| Gourdine, Meredith C. | Method and apparatus for converting chemical and thermal energy into electricity | April 10, 1990 | 4,916,033 |
| Gourdine, Meredith C. | Apparatus and method for cooling heat generating electronic components in a cabinet | March 22, 1994 | 5,297,005 |
| Gourdine, Meredith C. | Apparatus and method for cooling heat generating electronic components in a cabinet | June 6, 1995 | 5,422,787 |

| Inventor | Description of Invention | Date | Patent No. |
|---|---|---|---|
| Gourdine, Meredith C. | Method and apparatus for producing multivortex fluid flow | Oct. 10, 1995 | 5,456,596 |
| Gourdine, Meredith C. | Method and apparatus for converting chemical and thermal energy into electricity | Jan. 30, 1996 | 5,487,957 |
| Gourdine, Meredith C. | Method and apparatus for transferring heat, mass, and momentum between a fluid and a surface | Aug. 27, 1996 | 5,548,907 |
| Grant, George F. | Golf tee | Dec. 12, 1899 | 638,920 |
| Grant, William S. | Curtain rod support | Aug. 4, 1896 | 565,075 |
| Gray, Robert H. | Baling press | Aug. 28,1894 | 525,203 |
| Gray, Robert H. | Cistern cleaner | April 9, 1895 | 537,151 |
| Green, Harry James, Jr. | Method of making a striated support for filaments | Dec. 15, 1970 | 3,548,045 |
| Green, Harry James, Jr. | Substrate for mounting filaments in close-spaced parallel array | June 8, 1971 | 3,584,130 |

| Inventor | Description of Invention | Date | Patent No. |
|---|---|---|---|
| Green, Harry James, Jr. | Method for sealing microelectronic device packages | March 14, 1972 | 3,648,357 |
| Greene, Ervin G. | Guard for downspouts | Oct. 10, 1933 | 1,930.354 |
| Greene, Frank S., Jr. | Use of faulty storage circuits by position coding | April 4, 1972 | 3,654,610 |
| Gregg, Clarence | Machine gun | Aug. 27, 1918 | 1,277,307 |
| Gregory, James | Motor | April 26, 1887 | 361,937 |
| Grenon, Henry | Razor stopping device | Feb. 18, 1896 | 554,867 |
| Griffin, Bessie Virginia | Portable receptacle support | April 24, 1951 | 2,550,554 |
| Griffin, Michael D. | Progressive throttle positioning system | Oct. 9, 1984 | 4,476,068 |
| Griffin, Michael D. | Throttle return spring assembly | March 18, 1986 | 4,576,762 |
| Griffin, Thomas Walter | Pool table attachment | June 13, 1899 | 626,902 |
| Grimes, Hermon L. | Airplane, folding wings | Nov. 22, 1938 | 2,137,486 |

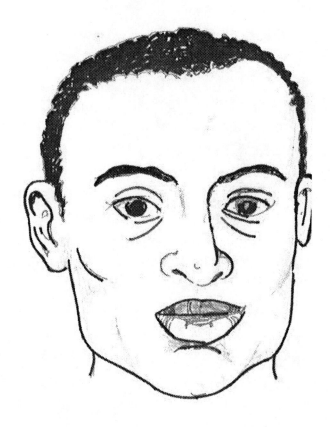

# Claude Harvard developed a method to make metal used in automobiles thinner and stronger

Claude Harvard was born in 1911. He was an automotive engineer when he exhibited some of his marvelous devices at the 1934 World's Fair in Chicago. Harvard was considered a 23-year-old automotive genius that worked for Ford Motor Company. It was while he was attending the Henry Ford Trade School that he came to the attention of Henry Ford. Mr. Ford asked the young man to fix a radio that had been giving him trouble. Soon, Harvard was part on elite group of men who worked at the Ford Experimental Laboratory developing machinery that would make the manufacturing of automobiles easier and more efficient. Harvard came into national prominence when he developed a method that helped roll metal so that it was thinner and stronger. While attending a ceremony at Tuskegee Institute he met Dr. George Washington Carver. The *Wizard of Tuskegee* was so impressed with Harvard he offered him the opportunity to work in his laboratory. Harvard later served as the catalyst for a meeting between Dr. Carver and Henry Ford.

## AFRICAN AMERICAN INVENTORS

| Inventor | Description of Invention | Date | Patent No. |
|----------|--------------------------|------|------------|
| Gunn, Selim W. | Shoe | Jan. 16, 1900 | 641,642 |
| Gurley, Clyde Edward | Automatic telephone alarm apparatus | April 7, 1970 | 3,505,476 |
| Gurley, Clyde Edward | Programmable external dial operating device | April 7, 1970 | 3,505,483 |
| Haines, James Henry | Portable shampooing basin | Sept. 28, 1897 | 590,833 |
| Hale, William | Motor vehicle | June 5, 1928 | 1,672,212 |
| Hale, William | Aeroplane | Nov. 24, 1925 | 1,563,278 |
| Hall, Lloyd Augustus | Asphalt emulsion and manufacture thereof | Oct. 18, 1932 | 1,882,834 |
| Hall, Lloyd Augustus | Protective coating | June 13, 1933 | 1,914,351 |
| Hall, Lloyd Augustus | Solid seasoning composition containing capsicum and chloride | March 19, 1935 | 1,995,119 |
| Hall, Lloyd Augustus | Nonbleaching solid seasoning composition | March 19, 1935 | 1,995,120 |

# Cornelius Henderson was the structural steel design engineer for the Ambassador Bridge and the Detroit-Windsor tunnels

Cornelius Langston Henderson was born in 1888 and he became one of the most prominent construction engineers in the country. Henderson was the second black to receive an engineering degree from the University of Michigan. The success of many major projects was due in part to the work of Cornelius Henderson. Such projects as the bridge that spans the Detroit River and the tunnels that go under the river's bed are architectural and engineering marvels, for not only must they fulfill the practical needs of the cars and trucks that use them, they must not interfere with the shipping traffic. Henderson joined the Canadian Bridge Company in 1911 and remained there until he retired in 1958. He worked on projects that included the General Electric Building in Toronto and the Detroit Memorial Park. Perhaps his most memorable assignment was as a structural steel designer for the Ambassador Bridge and the Detroit-Windsor Tunnels. Henderson died in 1976.

## AFRICAN AMERICAN INVENTORS

| Inventor | Description of Invention | Date | Patent No. |
|---|---|---|---|
| Hall, Lloyd Augustus | Stabilized solid seasoning composition | March 19, 1935 | 1,995,121 |
| Hall, Lloyd Augustus | Vitamin concentrate | Nov. 26, 1935 | 2,022,464 |
| Hall, Lloyd Augustus | Solid seasoning composition containing lecithin | March 3, 1936 | 2,032,612 |
| Hall, Lloyd Augustus | Manufacture of bleached pepper products | Oct. 26, 1937 | 2,097,405 |
| Hall, Lloyd Augustus and Griffith, Carroll L. | Sterilizing foodstuffs | Feb. 8, 1938 | 2,107,697 |
| Hall, Lloyd Augustus | Curing of meats and the like | May 17, 1938 | 2,117478 |
| Hall, Lloyd Augustus | Alkaline detergent compound | Jan. 3, 1939 | 2,142,870 |
| Hall, Lloyd Augustus | Homogeneous alkaline detergents and method of producing same | Jan. 3, 1939 | 2,142,871 |
| Hall, Lloyd Augustus | Stabilized nitrite salt composition | Jan. 31, 1939 | 2,145,417 |
| Hall, Lloyd Augustus | Inhibited detergent composition | April 18, 1939 | 2,155,045 |

| Inventor | Description of Invention | Date | Patent No. |
|---|---|---|---|
| Hall, Lloyd Augustus | Inhibited detergent composition | April 18, 1939 | 2,155,046 |
| Hall, Lloyd Augustus | Manufacture of protein composition | April 25, 1939 | 2,155,417 |
| Hall, Lloyd Augustus | Composition of matter | Aug. 29, 1939 | 2,171,428 |
| Hall, Lloyd Augustus | Sterilization process | Feb. 13, 1940 | 2,189,947 |
| Hall, Lloyd Augustus | Edible dusting powder | Jan. 17, 1939 | 2,144,371 |
| Hall, Lloyd Augustus | Composition of matter | Aug. 29, 1939 | 1,171,428 |
| Hall, Lloyd Augustus | Sterilization process | Feb. 13, 1940 | 2,189,947 |
| Hall, Lloyd Augustus | Sterilization of pancreatin | Feb. 13, 1940 | 2,189,948 |
| Hall, Lloyd Augustus | Sterilization colloid materials | Feb. 13, 1940 | 2,189,949 |
| Hall, Lloyd Augustus | Protein composition of matter | Aug. 5, 1941 | 2,251,334 |

| Inventor | Description of Invention | Date | Patent No. |
|---|---|---|---|
| Hall, Lloyd Augustus | Seasoning material derived from red peppers and the derivation thereof | Oct. 28, 1941 | 2,260,897 |
| Hall, Lloyd Augustus | Sterilization process | March 9, 1943 | RE 22,284 |
| Hall, Lloyd Augustus | Yeast food | June 15, 1943 | 2,321,673 |
| Hall, Lloyd Augustus | Puncture sealing composition and manufacture thereof | Sept. 5, 1944 | 2,357,650 |
| Hall, Lloyd Augustus | Manufacture of nitrogen-fortified whey concentrate | Nov. 28, 1944 | 2,363,730 |
| Hall, Lloyd Augustus | Capsicum-containing seasoning composition | Sept. 25, 1945 | 2,385,412 |
| Hall, Lloyd Augustus | Production of protein hydrolysate flavoring material | Jan. 14, 1947 | 2,414,299 |
| Hall, Lloyd Augustus | Manufacture of stable dry papain composition | March 15, 1949 | 2,464,200 |
| Hall, Lloyd Augustus | Antioxidant | March 22, 1949 | 2,464,927 |

# Dr. Mae Jemison, a physician, chemical engineer and professor, became the first African American woman astronaut in 1987

When she was growing up, Mae Jemison was afraid of heights. She not only conquered her fear but countless other obstacles to become a physician, chemical engineer, Ivy League professor and astronaut when she ventured into space in her historical first flight aboard the Space Shuttle Endeavor in 1992. In the mid-1980s, NASA's crew of astronauts included African Americans and women, but no African American women. Dr. Mae Jemison made it her business to correct that deficiency. She applied to NASA and was accepted for astronaut training in 1987. She now teaches at Dartmouth College in New Hampshire and runs an academic camp in Houston that encourages children to enter the science fields. Dr. Mae Jemison is a great role model for all Americans.

# AFRICAN AMERICAN INVENTORS

| Inventor | Description of Invention | Date | Patent No. |
|----------|--------------------------|------|------------|
| Hall, Lloyd Augustus | Phospholipoid carrier for antioxidant | March 22, 1949 | 2,464,928 |
| Hall, Lloyd Augustus | Gelatin-base coating for food and the like | Aug. 2, 1949 | 2,477,742 |
| Hall, Lloyd Augustus | Synergistic antioxidants and the methods of preparing the same | Jan. 3, 1950 | 2,493,288 |
| Hall, Lloyd Augustus | Antioxidant | March 14, 1950 | 2,500,543 |
| Hall, Lloyd Augustus | Synergistic antioxidant | June 13, 1950 | 2,511,802 |
| Hall, Lloyd Augustus | Antioxidant flakes | June 13, 1950 | 2,511,803 |
| Hall, Lloyd Augustus | Antioxidant salt | June 13, 1950 | 2,511,804 |
| Hall, Lloyd Augustus | Synergistic antioxidant containing amino acids | Aug. 8, 1950 | 2,518,233 |
| Hall, Lloyd Augustus | Production of protein hydrolysate | Jan. 2, 1951 | 2,536,171 |
| Hall, Lloyd Augustus | Antioxidant | Jan. 16, 1951 | RE 23,329 |
| Hall, Lloyd Augustus | Curing process for bacon | May 15, 1951 | 2,553,533 |

| Inventor | Description of Invention | Date | Patent No. |
|---|---|---|---|
| Hall, Lloyd Augustus | Spice extraction and product | Oct. 16, 1951 | 2,571,867 |
| Hall, Lloyd Augustus | Spice extract and method of producing | Oct. 16, 1951 | 2,571,948 |
| Hall, Lloyd Augustus | Manufacture of meat-curing composition | Feb. 9, 1954 | 2,668,770 |
| Hall, Lloyd Augustus | Stable curing salt composition and manufacture thereof | Feb. 9, 1954 | 2,668,771 |
| Hall, Lloyd Augustus | Synergistic antioxidants containing antioxidant acids | May 4, 1954 | 2,677,616 |
| Hall, Lloyd Augustus | Antioxidant composition | Aug. 14, 1956 | 2,758,931 |
| Hall, Lloyd Augustus | Reaction product of polyoxyethylene derivative of a fatty acid partial ester of hexitol anhydride and citric acid and an antioxidant containing the same | Sept. 4, 1956 | 2,761,784 |

| Inventor | Description of Invention | Date | Patent No. |
|---|---|---|---|
| Hall, Lloyd Augustus | Meat-curing salt composition | Nov. 13, 1956 | 2,770,548 |
| Hall, Lloyd Augustus | Meat-curing salt composition | Nov. 13, 1956 | 2,770,549 |
| Hall, Lloyd Augustus | Meat-curing salt composition | Nov. 13, 1956 | 2,770,550 |
| Hall, Lloyd Augustus | Meat-curing salt composition | Nov. 13, 1956 | 2,770,551 |
| Hall, Lloyd Augustus | Antioxidant material and use of said material in treating meat | Nov. 27, 1956 | 2,772,169 |
| Hall, Lloyd Augustus | Antioxidant composition | Nov. 27, 1956 | 2,772,170 |
| Hall, Lloyd Augustus | Fatty monoglyceride citrate and anti-oxidant containing the same | Nov. 12, 1957 | 2,813,032 |
| Hall, Lloyd Augustus | Method of preserving fresh frozen pork trimmings | July 29, 1958 | 2,845,358 |
| Hall, Lloyd Augustus | Sterilization of hospital and physicians' supplies | May 31, 1960 | 2,938,766 |
| Hall, Lloyd Augustus | Antioxidant composition | April 25, 1961 | 2,981,628 |

| Inventor | Description of Invention | Date | Patent No. |
|---|---|---|---|
| Hall, Virginia E. | Embroided fruit bowl wall hanging | April 5, 1977 | 4,016,314 |
| Hammonds, Julia Terry | Apparatus for holding yarn skeins | Dec. 15, 1896 | 572,985 |
| Harding, Felix Harding | Extension banquet table | Nov. 22, 1898 | 614,468 |
| Harney, Michael C. | Lantern or lamp | Aug. 19 , 1884 | 303,844 |
| Harper, David | Mobile utility rack | April 12, 1960 | D 187,654 |
| Harper, David | Bookcase | June 6, 1961 | D 190,500 |
| Harper, Solomon | Electrical hair treating implement | Aug. 5, 1930 | 1,772,002 |
| Harper, Solomon | Thermostatic controlled hair curlers, comb, and irons | Aug. 11, 1953 | 2,648,757 |
| Harper, Solomon | Thermostatic controlled fur and material dressing equipment | June 21, 1955 | 2,711,095 |
| Harris, Betty W. | Spot test for 1,3,5-triamino-2,4,6-trinitrobenzene TATB | Oct. 21, 1986 | 4,618,452 |

| Inventor | Description of Invention | Date | Patent No. |
|---|---|---|---|
| Harris, Edward L. | Apparatus for handling corrosive acid substances | July 24, 1956 | 2,756,129 |
| Harrison, Emmett Scott | Gas turbine air compressor and control therefore | Sept. 21, 1971 | 3,606,971 |
| Harrison, Emmett Scott | Turbojet afterburner engine with two-position exhaust nozzle | Jan. 6, 1981 | 4,242,865 |
| Harrison, Jesse | Combination tooth brush and paste holder | Feb. 9, 1932 | 1,844,036 |
| Harwell, William D. | Apparatus and method of capturing an orbiting spacecraft | May 12, 1987 | 4,664,344 |
| Hawkins, Joseph | Gridiron | March 26, 1845 | 3,973 |
| Hawkins, Randall | Harness attachment | Oct. 4, 1887 | 370,943 |
| Hawkins, Walter Lincoln | Preparation of 1,2, Di-Primary amines | Feb. 26, 1952 | 2,587,043 |
| Hawkins, Walter Lincoln | Stabilized straight-chain hydrocarbons | June 2, 1959 | 2,889,306 |

| Inventor | Description of Invention | Date | Patent No. |
|---|---|---|---|
| Hawkins, Walter Lincoln | Stabilized alpha-mono-olefinic polymers | Feb. 14, 1967 | 3,304,283 |
| Headen, Minnis | Foot power hammer | Oct. 5, 1886 | 350,363 |
| Hearns, Robert | Sealing attachment for bottles | Feb. 15, 1898 | 598,929 |
| Hearns, Robert | Detachable car fender | July 4, 1899 | 628,003 |
| Hearns, William | Device for removing and inserting taps and plugs in water mains | Oct. 8, 1912 | 1,040,538 |
| Helm, Tony W. | Universal joint | Aug. 28, 1956 | 2,760,358 |
| Henderson, Henry Fairfax, Jr. | Weight loss control system | Sept. 5, 1978 | 4,111,336 |
| Hill, Henry Aaron | Manufacture of azodicarbonamide | June 13, 1961 | 2,988,545 |
| Hill, Henry Aaron | Foamable composition comprising a thermoplastic polymer and barium azocarbonate and method of foaming | July 14, 1964 | 3,141,002 |

| Inventor | Description of Invention | Date | Patent No. |
|----------|------------------------|------|------------|
| Hill, Henry Aaron | Curing furfuryl-alcohol-modified urea formaldehyde condensates | Jan. 10, 1967 | 3,297,611 |
| Hilyer, Andrew F. | Water evaporator attachment for hot air registers | Aug. 26, 1890 | 435,095 |
| Hilyer, Andrew F. | Evaporator for hot air registers | Oct. 14, 1890 | 438,159 |
| Hines, Samuel J. | Life preserver | May 14, 1915 | 1,137,971 |
| Hines, Samuel J. | Lawn mower attachment | May 30, 1933 | 1,911,278 |
| Hodge, John E. | Novel reductones and methods of making them (Hodge has numerous patents in the field of food technology. | May 10, 1960 | 2,936,308 |
| Hodge, John E. | Glucose-amine sequestrants | Aug. 15,1961 | 2,996,449 |
| Hodge, John E. | Substituted benzodioxan sweetening compound | March 27, 1979 | 4,146,650 |

| Inventor | Description of Invention | Date | Patent No. |
|---|---|---|---|
| Hodges, Clarence B. and McCoy, Elijah | Lubricator | Nov. 18, 1884 | 308,258 |
| Holmes, Elijah H. | Gage | Nov. 12, 1865 | 549,513 |
| Holmes, Lydia M. | Knockdown wheeled toy | Nov. 14, 1950 | 2,529,692 |
| Hopkins, Harry C. | Power controller | Nov. 3, 1987 | 4,704,570 |
| Horne, June B. | Emergency escape apparatus and method of using same | Feb. 12, 1985 | 4,498,557 |
| Howard, Darnley E. | Optical apparatus for indicating the position of a tool | Jan. 24, 1939 | 2,145,116 |
| Howard, Darnley Moseley | Method of making radome with an integral antenna | June 24, 1969 | 3,451,127 |
| Hughes, Isaiah D. | Combined excavator and elevator | Nov. 26, 1901 | 687,312 |
| Hull, Wilson E. | Sublimation timing switch | Nov. 15, 1966 | 3,286,064 |
| Hull, Wilson E. | Mass release mechanism for satellites | Jan. 28, 1969 | 3,424,403 |

| Inventor | Description of Invention | Date | Patent No. |
|----------|--------------------------|------|------------|
| Hunter, John W. | Portable weighing scale | Nov. 3, 1896 | 570,553 |
| Huntley, James E. | Emergency fire escape mechanism | April 29, 1975 | 3,880,255 |
| Hyde, Robert N. | Composition for cleaning and preserving carpets | Nov. 6 1888 | 392,205 |
| Ingram, Clifton M. | Railroad crossing flag signal | Feb. 10, 1925 | 1,526,215 |
| Ingram, Clifton M. | Well drilling tool | June 16, 1925 | 1,542,776 |
| Jackson, Benjamin F. | Heating apparatus | March 1, 1898 | 599,985 |
| Jackson, Benjamin F. | Matrix drying apparatus | May 10, 1898 | 603,879 |
| Jackson, Benjamin F. | Gas burner | April 4, 1899 | 622,482 |
| Jackson, Benjamin F. | Steam boiler | Jan. 7, 1902 | 690,730 |
| Jackson, Brian G. | Portable highway warning device with frangible retainer ring | July 7, 1998 | 5,775,834 |

| Inventor | Description of Invention | Date | Patent No. |
| --- | --- | --- | --- |
| Jackson, Harry | Advertising apparatus | June 28, 1932 | 1,865,374 |
| Jackson, Harry and Jackson, Mary E. | Protective appliance | April 21, 1936 | 2,038,491 |
| Jackson, Harry and Jackson, Mary E. | Protective appliance | Sept. 1, 1936 | 2,053,035 |
| Jackson, Harry and Jackson, Mary E. | Burglar alarm switch | Feb. 23, 1937 | 2,071,343 |
| Jackson, Henry | Method and composition for autocatalytically depositing copper | April 1, 1969 | 3,436,233 |
| Jackson, Henry A. | Kitchen table | Oct. 6, 1896 | 569,135 |
| Jackson, Norman | Pneumatic tire | July 12, 1921 | 1,384,134 |
| Jackson, William H. | Railway switch | March 9, 1897 | 578,641 |
| Jackson, William H. | Railway switch | Nov. 16, 1897 | 593,665 |
| Jackson, William H. | Automatic locking switch | Aug. 23, 1898 | 609,436 |

# Dr. Anthony Johnson's experiments with pulses of laser light has advanced the optical properties of glass fibers for the ultimate in communications

Anthony Johnson knew what he wanted to do when his parents gave him a chemistry set while he was in the fourth grade. He wanted a career in science. He followed that goal when he was granted his Ph.D. by the City University of New York in 1981. He became a member of AT&T Bell Laboratories in Holmdel, New Jersey. Johnson considers the highlight of his career was the opportunity he had to co-chair the 1992 Conference on Lasers and Electro-Optics, the world's largest laser meeting with over 7,000 in attendance. At Bell Laboratories, Johnson researches lasers and fiber optics, seeking to make quantum gains in communications technology. He realizes that by using the nearly limitless capacity of optical fiber, a system can transmit as many as 600,000 phone conversations simultaneously. Dr. Johnson believes that the future in communications is wide open and the key to high capacity is the laser's pulse rate. He also strongly feels that one-day people will have access to entire libraries directly from their home telephones, computers, and television systems placing a world of information at their fingertips.

# In 1908, the flamboyant and powerful Jack Johnson became the first black heavyweight champion of the boxing world and later, in 1922, the U.S. Patent Office issued him a patent for inventing the wrench

Jack Arthur Johnson became the first black heavyweight boxing champion of the world in 1908 by defeating Tommy Burns in Sydney, Australia. He knocked out Burns in the fourteenth round. A few years later, he became a prison inmate, victim of a law used to prevent a black man from traveling with a white woman. He was sentenced to one year at a federal prison in Leavenworth, Kansas. There, with time on his hands and work to do, Johnson created a tool to tighten and loosen fastening devices. As a result he was granted a U.S. Patent for inventing the hand wrench. Later, he was also granted a patent for inventing a theft prevention device for vehicles. Johnson died in 1946.

## AFRICAN AMERICAN INVENTORS

| Inventor | Description of Invention | Date | Patent No. |
|---|---|---|---|
| Jefferson, Donald E. | Triggered exploding wire device | Nov. 29, 1966 | 3,288,068 |
| Jefferson, Donald E. | Digital data storage system | July 18, 1972 | 3,678,468 |
| Jennings, Thomas L. | Dry scouring (first patent granted to an African American). | March 3, 1821 | 3306X |
| Johnson, Andrew R. | Precision digital delay circuit | April 2, 1968 | 3,376,436 |
| Johnson, Anthony M. | Photodetector having semi-insulating material and a contoured substantially periodic surface | Nov. 26, 1985 | 4,555,622 |
| Johnson, Anthony M. | Integrated optical device having integral photodetector | Nov. 3, 1987 | 4,703,996 |
| Johnson, Anthony M. | High speed circuit measurements using photoemission sampling | Jan. 26, 1988 | 4,721,910 |
| Johnson, Daniel | Rotary dining table | Jan. 15, 1889 | 396,089 |

| Inventor | Description of Invention | Date | Patent No. |
|---|---|---|---|
| Johnson, Daniel | Lawn mower attachment | Sept. 10, 1889 | 410,836 |
| Johnson, Daniel | Grass receiver for lawn mowers | June 10, 1890 | 429,629 |
| Johnson, George M. | Automatic stopping and releasing device for mine cars | Dec. 4, 1917 | 1,249,106 |
| Johnson, Isaac R. | Bicycle frame | Oct. 10, 1899 | 634,823 |
| Johnson, John Arthur (First African American heavyweight boxing champion) | Wrench | April 18, 1922 | 1,413,121 |
| Johnson, John Arthur | Theft-preventing device for vehicles | Dec. 12, 1922 | 1,438,709 |
| Johnson, Lonnie G. | Digital distance measuring instrument | May 6, 1979 | 4,143,267 |
| Johnson, Lonnie G. | Variable resistance type sensor controlled switch | Jan. 1, 1980 | 4,181,843 |
| Johnson, Lonnie G. | Smoke detecting timer controlled thermostat | July 8, 1980 | 4,211,362 |

# General Daniel "Chappie" James became the first black four star general in U.S. history in August of 1975, as Commander-In-Chief of NORAD

In August 1975, General Daniel "Chappie" James of the U.S. Air Force became the nation's first African American four-star general. He was also named commander of the North American Air Defense Command (NORAD) at Peterson Air Force Base in Colorado. In this capacity, he was responsible for all U.S. and Canadian strategic aerospace defense forces. James was born in Pensacola, Florida in 1920. He was the youngest of seventeen children. He attended Tuskegee Institute and received a degree in physical education, but then completed pilot training under the Civilian Pilot Training Program. He was asked to remain at Tuskegee as an instructor pilot in the Army Air Corps Aviation Cadet Program. He later entered the program as a cadet and received his commission as a second lieutenant in 1943. By 1949 James was stationed at Clark Field in the Philippines. In Korea, in 1950, he flew 101 missions. From 1957 to 1966, James attended the Air Command and Staff College. He was then reassigned to Headquarters U.S. Air Force, the Pentagon; to the Royal Air Force Station at Bentwaters, England and to David-Monthan Air Force Base in Arizona. When the Vietnam War began, James was assigned to Ubon Royal Thai Air Force Base in Thailand, in 1966, where he flew 78 combat missions into North Vietnam. He led a flight in which seven MiG-21s were knocked from the skies. The highest kill of any mission during the Vietnam War. In 1970, he served as deputy assistant. secretary of defense and in 1974 he served as vice commander of the Military Airlift Command. General "Chappie" James retired on February 1, 1978 and in less than four weeks on February 25 he died.

## AFRICAN AMERICAN INVENTORS

| Inventor | Description of Invention | Date | Patent No. |
|---|---|---|---|
| Johnson, Lonnie G. | Automatic sprinkler control | March 3, 1981 | 4,253,606 |
| Johnson, Lonnie G. | Thermal energy accumulation | Oct. 16, 1984 | 4,476,693 |
| Johnson, Lonnie G. | Soil moisture potential determination by weight measurement | April 9, 1985 | 4,509,361 |
| Johnson, Lonnie G. | Squirt gun | May 27, 1986 | 4,591,071 |
| Johnson, Lonnie G. | Johnson tube, a thermodynamic heat pump | Feb. 16, 1988 | 4,724,683 |
| Johnson, Lonnie G. | Flow actuated pulsator | July 19, 1988 | 4,757,946 |
| Johnson, Lonnie G. | Pinch trigger pump water gun | Dec. 24, 1991 | 5,074,437 |
| Johnson, Lonnie G. | Double tank pinch trigger pump water gun | Sept. 29, 1992 | 5,150,819 |
| Johnson, Lonnie G. | Liquid jet propelled transporter and launcher toy | March 30, 1993 | 5,197,452 |

| Inventor | Description of Invention | Date | Patent No. |
|---|---|---|---|
| Johnson, Lonnie G. | Pinch trigger hand pump water gun with multiple tanks | Aug. 24, 1993 | 5,238,149 |
| Johnson, Lonnie G. | Wet diaper detector | Nov. 30, 1993 | 5,266,928 |
| Johnson, Lonnie G. | Combined aerodynamic glider and launcher | Dec. 21, 1993 | D 342,551 |
| Johnson, Lonnie G. | Pinch trigger water gun with rearwardly mounted hand pump | March 8, 1994 | 5,292,032 |
| Johnson, Lonnie G. | Hair drying curler apparatus | April 5, 1994 | 5,299,367 |
| Johnson, Lonnie G. | Pinch trigger hand pump water gun with non-detachable tank | April 26, 1994 | 5,305,919 |
| Johnson, Lonnie G. | Low pressure, high volume pressurized water gun | June 21, 1994 | 5,322,191 |
| Johnson, Lonnie G. | Water arrow projecting bow | July 26, 1994 | 5,332,120 |
| Johnson, Lonnie G. | Pressurized toy rocket with rapid action release mechanism | Jan. 17, 1995 | 5,381,778 |

# NASA scientist, Katherine G. Johnson, developed a mathematical method to keep track of a space ship when it was out of Earth's atmosphere

Without the work of dedicated scientists like Katherine G. Johnson, humans would never have walked on the moon. Born in 1918, Johnson received her initial training as a physicist and mathematician in her native West Virginia. It was there she became interested in working on the space program. In 1960, as part of a scientific team at the National Aeronautics and Space Administration (NASA) Langley Research Center in Hampton, Virginia, Johnson made one of the most significant contributions to early space flight. She developed a new mathematical method whereby scientists could keep track of a spaceship every minute it was out of Earth's atmosphere. In the mid-seventies she further extended her outstanding work by interpreting data from secret pilotless aircraft which was in actuality, prototype spacecraft, in preparation for the Apollo Moon Landing project. Johnson has also worked on many other fascinating projects including the development of a satellite that would take pictures of the Earth and help fine minerals located under the soil. For her innovative vision and tremendous contributions she was named the recipient of the Group Achievement Award presented to NASA's Lunar Space Craft and Operations Team.

# AFRICAN AMERICAN INVENTORS

| Inventor | Description of Invention | Date | Patent No. |
|---|---|---|---|
| Johnson, Lonnie G. | Toy airplane and launcher | March 7, 1995 | 5,395,275 |
| Johnson, Lonnie G. | Fluid pulsator with accumulator for frequency control | March 21, 1995 | 5,398,873 |
| Johnson, Lonnie G. | Toy rocket with velocity dependent chute release | April 18, 1995 | 5,407,375 |
| Johnson, Lonnie G. | Pressurized air/water rocket and launcher | May 16, 1995 | 5,415,153 |
| Johnson, Lonnie G. | Wet diaper detector | Nov. 21, 1995 | 5,469,145 |
| Johnson, Lonnie G. | Fluid powering and launching system for a toy vehicle | March 19, 1996 | 5,499,940 |
| Johnson, Lonnie G. | Air pressure toy rocket launcher | July 23, 1996 | 5,538,453 |
| Johnson, Lonnie G. | Thermionic generator | July 30, 1996 | 5,541,464 |
| Johnson, Lonnie G. | Toy rocket with velocity dependent chute release | Aug. 27, 1996 | 5,549,497 |

*Donald and Jane Wilson*

# Lonnie Johnson is a nuclear and mechanical engineer who has invented toys such as the popular *Super Soaker* to generate capital to develop more complex devices

Lonnie Johnson, a nuclear and mechanical engineer, has spent years at NASA. While there, he helped develop thermodynamic and control systems for space projects, including those for the Galileo Jupiter probe and the Mars Observer project. Johnson now operates his own research and development company and he has also invented the popular *Super Soaker* toy water gun. He said he got the idea for the water toy while experimenting with a new heat pump for refrigerators that would use water and eliminate the need for Freon. Like so many African American inventors, Johnson said it was difficult to get financial support to develop many more serious inventions. The sale of his popular toys such as the

Super Soaker and the Nerf Wildfire dart gun has financed his other experiments. Johnson said he finds personal satisfaction in knowing he can make his ideas reality, but he also wants young people to know about what inventions he created. In this book alone, Johnson has more than 40 U.S. Patents. Johnson says, "It is my responsibility to let young people know an African American is responsible for so many creations. If there are kids who need strong role models and who need confidence to be able to believe in themselves, then as a proud African American, I want to be able to be that role model and help boost their self-esteem."

# AFRICAN AMERICAN INVENTORS

| Inventor | Description of Invention | Date | Patent No. |
|---|---|---|---|
| Johnson, Lonnie G. | Pneumatic launcher for a toy projectile and the like | Sept. 10, 1996 | 5,553,598 |
| Johnson, Lonnie G. | Electric pump toy water gun | Dec. 24, 1996 | 5,586,688 |
| Johnson, Lonnie G. | Double tank pinch trigger pump water gun | Dec. 31, 1996 | RE 35,412 |
| Johnson, Lonnie G. | Compressed air gun with magazine indexer | Jan. 14, 1997 | 5,592,931 |
| Johnson, Lonnie G. | Rapid fire compressed air gun | Jan. 28, 1997 | 5,596,978 |
| Johnson, Lonnie G. | Compressed air gun | May 6, 1997 | 5,626,123 |
| Johnson, Lonnie G. | Toy rocket launcher | Aug. 5, 1997 | 5,653,216 |
| Johnson, Lonnie G. | Rapid fire compressed air gun | Dec. 23, 1997 | 5,699,781 |
| Johnson, Lonnie G. | Compressed air gun with single action pump | Dec. 30, 1997 | 5,701,879 |
| Johnson, Lonnie G. | System for detonating a percussion cap in a toy projectile | Jan. 13, 1998 | 5,707,270 |

| Inventor | Description of Invention | Date | Patent No. |
|----------|-------------------------|------|------------|
| Johnson, Lonnie G. | Rapid fire compressed air gun (Super Soaker). | Jan. 20, 1998 | 5,709,199 |
| Johnson, Lonnie G. | Hair drying curler apparatus | Jan. 27, 1998 | 5,711,324 |
| Johnson, Lonnie G. | Voice activated compressed air toy gun | March 10, 1998 | 5,724,955 |
| Johnson, Paul E. | Therapeutic lamps | Jan. 19, 1932 | 1,842,100 |
| Johnson, Payton | Swinging chair | Nov. 15, 1881 | 249,530 |
| Johnson, Powell | Eye protector | Nov. 2, 1880 | 234,039 |
| Johnson, Wesley | Velocipede | June 20, 1899 | 627,335 |
| Johnson, William A. | Paint vehicle | Dec. 4, 1888 | 393,763 |
| Johnson, Willie Harry | Mechanism for overcoming dead centers | Feb. 4, 1896 | 554,223 |
| Johnson, Willie Harry | Mechanism for overcoming dead centers | Oct. 11, 1898 | 612,345 |

| Inventor | Description of Invention | Date | Patent No. |
|---|---|---|---|
| Johnson, Willis | Egg beater | Feb. 5, 1884 | 292,821 |
| Jones, Albert A. and Long, Amos E. | Caps for bottles, jars, etc. | Sept. 13, 1898 | 610,715 |
| Jones, Clinton | Electric release for toy guns | June 21, 1949 | 2,474,054 |
| Jones, Felix B. | Firearm | Sept. 25, 1928 | 1,685,673 |
| Jones, Frederick McKinley | Ticket dispensing machine | June 27, 1939 | 2,163,754 |
| Jones, Frederick McKinley | Design for air conditioning unit | April 28, 1942 | D 132,182 |
| Jones, Frederick McKinley | Removable cooling units for compartments | Dec. 14, 1943 | 2,336,735 |
| Jones, Frederick McKinley | Means for automatically stopping and starting gas engines | Dec. 21, 1943 | 2,337,164 |
| Jones, Frederick McKinley | Two-cycle gas engine | May 29, 1945 | 2,376,968 |
| Jones, Frederick McKinley | Two-cycle gas engine | March 11, 1947 | 2,417,253 |

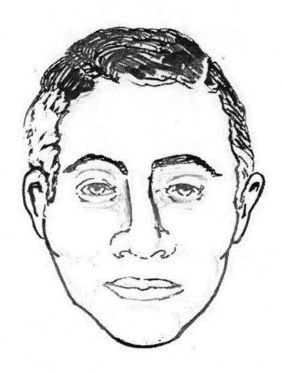

# Frederick M. Jones was the inventor of the air conditioning unit, refrigerated trucks, and the control device for internal combustion engines

Frederick M. Jones was a refrigeration pioneer who was born in 1892. He first came into prominence when he invented a machine that helped adapt silent film projectors to the new "talkies" in the late 1920s. He also designed the machine that delivers tickets and gives change when you pay your way into a theatre. However, it was his work with refrigeration that is considered his most important. He saw the need for keeping things cool and portable while he served in the army during World War I. When he came home he began to work on devices that would ultimately serve as field hospital refrigerators and portable x-ray machines. In 1935, he took his inventions and adapted them to the ever-increasing number of trucks that were just beginning to crisscross the nation. Jones received more than 60 U.S. Patents and he is credited with being the man most responsible for our ability to ship food long distances, whether in trucks, railroad cars or on ships. He also invented the air conditioner for vehicles. In 1943, Jones invented the self-starting gasoline engine. In 1958, Frederick M. Jones invented the control device for internal combustion engines. One of the most creative and resourceful inventors of his time, he died in 1961.

# AFRICAN AMERICAN INVENTORS

| Inventor | Description of Invention | Date | Patent No. |
|---|---|---|---|
| Jones, Frederick McKinley | Removable cooling unit for compartments | May 11, 1948 | RE 23,000 |
| Jones, Frederick McKinley | Means for preventing frosting of evaporator heat exchangers | May 31, 1949 | 2,471,692 |
| Jones, Frederick McKinley | Air conditioning unit (Jones' inventions made it possible to refrigerate trucks) | July 12, 1949 | 2,475,841 |
| Jones, Frederick McKinley | Starter generator | July 12, 1949 | 2,475,842 |
| Jones, Frederick McKinley | Means operated by a starter generator for cooling a gas engine | July 12, 1949 | 2,475,843 |
| Jones, Frederick McKinley | Means for thermostatically operating gas engines | July 26, 1949 | 2,477,377 |
| Jones, Frederick McKinley | Rotary compressor | April 18, 1950 | 2,504,841 |
| Jones, Frederick McKinley | System for controlling operation of refrigeration units | May 23, 1950 | 2,509,099 |
| Jones, Frederick McKinley | Air conditioning unit | July 4, 1950 | D 159,209 |

| Inventor | Description of Invention | Date | Patent No. |
|---|---|---|---|
| Jones, Frederick McKinley | Engine actuated ventilating system | Sept. 26, 1950 | 2,523,273 |
| Jones, Frederick McKinley | Apparatus for heating or cooling atmosphere within an enclosure | Oct. 24, 1950 | 2,526,874 |
| Jones, Frederick McKinley | Prefabricated refrigerator construction | Dec. 26, 1950 | 2,535,682 |
| Jones, Frederick McKinley | Refrigeration control device | Jan. 8, 1952 | 2,581,956 |
| Jones, Frederick McKinley | Locking mechanism | Aug. 4, 1953 | 2,647,287 |
| Jones, Frederick McKinley | Methods and means of defrosting a cold diffuser | Jan. 19, 1954 | 2,666,298 |
| Jones, Frederick McKinley | Method and means for air conditioning | Dec. 7, 1954 | 2,696,086 |
| Jones, Frederick McKinley | Method and means for preserving perishable foodstuffs in transit | Feb. 12, 1957 | 2,780,923 |
| Jones, Frederick McKinley | Control device for internal combustion engine | Sept. 2, 1958 | 2,850,001 |

| Inventor | Description of Invention | Date | Patent No. |
|---|---|---|---|
| Jones, Frederick McKinley | Thermostat and temperature control system | Feb. 23, 1960 | 2,926,005 |
| Jones, Howard St. Claire, Jr. | Antenna testing shield | April 10, 1962 | 3,029,430 |
| Jones, Howard St. Claire, Jr. | Waveguide components | July 24, 1962 | 3,046,507 |
| Jones, Howard St. Claire, Jr. | Reciprocal ferrite wave-guide phase shifter having means to rotate the magnetic field about an axis transverse to the longitudinal axis of the ferrite rod | Aug. 23, 1966 | 3,268,837 |
| Jones, Howard St. Claire, Jr. | Electronically scanned microwave antennas | Aug. 23, 1966 | 3,268,901 |
| Jones, Howard St. Claire, Jr. | Dielectric-loaded antenna with matching window | June 30, 1970 | 3,518,683 |
| Jones, Howard St. Claire, Jr. | Conformal edge-slot radiators | Sept. 27, 1977 | 4,051,480 |
| Jones, Howard St. Claire, Jr. | Multifrequency series-fed edge slot antenna | Dec. 8, 1981 | 4,305,078 |

| Inventor | Description of Invention | Date | Patent No. |
|---|---|---|---|
| Jones, James C. | Portable drill-frame | Jan. 22, 1895 | 532,881 |
| Jones, John Leslie | Preparation of substituted phenols | Feb. 14, 1950 | 2,497,503 |
| Jones, John Leslie | Personnel restraint system for vehicular occupants | Sept. 12, 1972 | 3,690,695 |
| Jones, John Leslie | Smokeless slow burning propellant | Sept. 12, 1978 | 4,112,849 |
| Jones, Sylvester S. | Manicuring device | Jan. 7, 1930 | 1,742,862 |
| Jones, Wilbert L. | Duplex capstan | June 28, 1966 | 3,258,247 |
| Jones, William B. | Dentist apparatus | `Oct. 19, 1937 | 2,096,375 |
| Jordan, John H. | Dresser | Feb. 16, 1971 | D 219,927 |
| Jordan, John H. | Cocktail table | May 18, 1971 | D 220, 768 |
| Jordan, John H. | Combined clock and wall plaque | June 22, 1971 | D 220,965 |

| Inventor | Description of Invention | Date | Patent No. |
|---|---|---|---|
| Joyce, James A. | Coal or ore bucket | April 26, 1898 | 603,143 |
| Joyner, Marjorie Stewart | Permanent waving machine (this patent was assigned to Madame C. J. Walker's company). | Nov. 27, 1928 | 1,693,515 |
| Julian, Hubert | Airplane safety appliance | May 24, 1921 | 1,379,264 |
| Julian, Percy Lavon | Recovery of sterols | Oct. 22, 1940 | 2,218,971 |
| Julian, Percy Lavon | Preparation of cortisone | June 26, 1956 | 2,752,339 |
| Julian, Percy Lavon | 16-Aminomenthyl-17-alkyltestosterone derivatives (Julian was a prolific researcher with over 100 patents worldwide) | Sept. 15, 1964 | 3,149,132 |
| Julian, Percy Lavon | Method for preparing 16 (alpha)-hydroxpregnenes and intermediates obtained therein | Sept. 20, 1966 | 3,274,178 |
| Julien, Leonard J. | Cane planter | Nov. 22, 1966 | 3,286,858 |

# Dr. Percy Lavon Julian contributed to the relief of pain and suffering for millions of people worldwide

In 1935, Dr. Percy Lavon Julian developed a new synthetic form of physostigmine, providing pain relief for millions of glaucoma sufferers all over the world. The grandson of a slave whose hand was mutilated because he learned how to read, Percy Lavon Julian, a famed chemist, physician and researcher was born in 1899 in Montgomery, Alabama. Julian received degrees at some of the most prestigious institutions in the world. A BA degree from DePauw University in 1920, a MA degree from Harvard University in 1923, and his Ph.D. degree from University of Vienna, Austria in 1931. He was an instructor at Fisk University from 1920 to 1925, won a fellowship to Harvard University in 1922, and was an instructor of chemistry at West Virginia State College. Julian became an associate professor of chemistry at Howard in 1927 where he established the chemistry building. Julian's brilliant career made him one of the leading chemists in America. He developed inexpensive copies of costly drugs, including synthetic male and female hormones which are used in treating cancer and were themselves the precursors to the development of birth control pills; and synthetic cortisone, a powerful painkiller for arthritis and other miseries of muscle and bone. Julian succeeded only through grim determination in face of massive racism. He also developed a synthetic progesterone, used to prevent miscarriages. Julian held 105 patents and founded Julian Laboratories in Chicago, Mexico City, and Guatemala. He was awarded the Spingarn Medal in 1947. Although later honored for a lifetime of achievements, Julian once could not take a job in Appleton, Wisconsin, because of a town law forbidding "the housing of a Negro overnight." Dr. Julian died in 1975.

## AFRICAN AMERICAN INVENTORS

| Inventor | Description of Invention | Date | Patent No. |
|---|---|---|---|
| Keelan, Harry Sanderlin | Colloidal silver iodide compound and method of preparing same | Dec. 2, 1930 | 1,783,334 |
| Kelley, George W. | Steam table | Oct. 26, 1897 | 592,591 |
| Kelly, Kenneth C. | Linearly polarized monopulse lobing antenna having cancellation of cross-polarization components in the principal lobe | Nov. 6, 1962 | 3,063,049 |
| Kelly, Lawrence Randolph | Programmable external dial operating device | April 7, 1970 | 3,505,483 |
| Kenner, Beatrice | Sanitary belt | May 15, 1956 | 2,745,406 |
| Kenner, Mary Beatrice | Carrier attachment for invalid walkers | May 18, 1976 | 3,957,071 |
| Kenner, Mary Beatrice | Bathroom tissue holder | Oct. 19, 1982 | 4,354,643 |
| Kenner, Mary Beatrice | Shower wall and bathtub mounted back washer | Sept. 29, 1987 | 4,696,068 |

| Inventor | Description of Invention | Date | Patent No. |
|---|---|---|---|
| King, James | Combination cotton thinning and cultivating machine | Feb. 28, 1928 | 1,661,122 |
| King, John G. | Power line sensing appliance theft alarm | Nov. 29, 1966 | 3,289,194 |
| Knox, Lawrence Howland | Production of arecoline | May 2, 1950 | 2,506,458 |
| Knox, Lawrence Howland | Photochemical preparation of tropilidenes | July 28, 1953 | ,647,081 |
| Knox, William J., Jr. | Coating aids for gelatin compositions | June 12, 1962 | 3,038,804 |
| Knox, William J., Jr. | Gelatin coating compositions (Knox has approximately 25 patents related to photography) | Feb. 28, 1967 | 3,306,749 |
| Knox, William J., Jr. | Coating aids for hydrophilic colloid layers of photographic elements | Nov. 10, 1970 | 3,539,352 |
| Latimer, Lewis Howard and Nichols, Joseph V. | Electric Lamp | Sept. 13, 1881 | 247,097 |

# In 1881, Lewis Howard Latimer was granted a U.S. Patent for inventing the first incandescent electric lamp with a carbon filament

Born in Chelsea, Massachusetts in 1848, Lewis H. Latimer, inventor, engineer and scientist, served in the Union Navy in 1863, studied drafting, and later invented and patented an incandescent light bulb with a carbon filament in 1881. After inventing the inexpensive process for making light bulb filaments, Latimer joined Thomas Edison's crack research team in 1884, where he distinguished himself in scientific inquiry and as an expert witness in patent lawsuits. He also served as an engineer for the Edison Company for many years and while he was with Edison, he supervised the installation of the electric light system in New York City, Philadelphia, Montreal, and London. Latimer was later employed by Alexander Graham Bell to make patent drawings for the first telephone. He also served as chief draftsman for General Electric and Westinghouse. He invented water closet (toilets) for railroad cars and a threaded wooden socket for light bulbs. A self-made genius, Latimer died in 1928.

## AFRICAN AMERICAN INVENTORS

| Inventor | Description of Invention | Date | Patent No. |
|---|---|---|---|
| Latimer, Lewis Howard | Process of manufacturing carbons | Jan. 17, 1882 | 252,386 |
| Latimer, Lewis Howard and Tregoning, John | Globe supporter for electric lamps | March 21, 1882 | 255,212 |
| Latimer, Lewis Howard and Brown, Charles W. | Water closets for railway cars | Feb. 10, 1874 | 147,363 |
| Latimer Lewis Howard | Apparatus for cooling and disinfecting | Jan. 12, 1886 | 334,078 |
| Latimer, Lewis Howard | Locking rack for hats, coats, and umbrellas | March 24, 1896 | 557, 076 |
| Latimer, Lewis Howard | Book supporter | Feb. 7, 1905 | 781,890 |
| Latimer, Lewis Howard | Lamp fixture (Latimer was one of the "Edison Pioneers" with patents in electricity) | Aug. 30, 1910 | 968,787 |
| Lavalette, William A. | Improvement in printing presses | Sept. 17, 1878 | 208,184 |
| Lavalette, William A. | Printing press (variation) | Sept. 17, 1878 | 208,208 |

# In 1907, Dr. Ernest E. Just became one of the most prominent biologist of his day at Dartmouth College

Ernest Everett Just was born in Charleston, S.C. in 1883. He attended Kimball Academy in New Hampshire and received a BA degree from Dartmouth College in 1907 and his Ph.D. degree in zoology and physiology from the University of Chicago in 1916. A biologist, zoologist, and educator, he was on the faculty of Howard University after 1907. Just said he could not understand why the NAACP had voted him the black man who had done the most to help his race. But the rest of the world understood. Just was one of the most outstanding biologists of his day. At Dartmouth College, Just's mind caught fire when he was introduced to biology, zoology and botany. He worked in the field of cellular research, documenting the origins of life and the intellectual capacity of human beings. He studied in Germany, Italy, and Woods Hole, Mass., an internationally recognized marine biological lab. Except for short leaves of absence, Just spent 20 summers at the laboratory in Woods Hole in research work and became a member of the ruling board. In 1930, he was the first black elected to serve as Vice President of the American Society of Zoologists. He published more than 50 papers in his field between 1912 and 1937. He made many discoveries that scientists are still studying today. Dr. Ernest E. Just died in 1941.

## AFRICAN AMERICAN INVENTORS

| Inventor | Description of Invention | Date | Patent No. |
| --- | --- | --- | --- |
| Lee, Arthur | Self propelled toy fish | Dec. 22, 1936 | 2,065,337 |
| Lee, Henry | Improvement in animal traps | Feb. 12, 1867 | 61,941 |
| Lee, Joseph | Kneading machine | Aug. 7, 1894 | 524,042 |
| Lee, Joseph | Bread crumbling machine | June 4, 1895 | 540,553 |
| Lee, Lester A. | Carbon dioxide laser fuels | March 8, 1977 | 4,011,116 |
| Lee, Maurice William | Aromatic pressure cooker and smoker | Sept. 29, 1959 | 2,906,191 |
| Lee, Robert | Safety attachment for automotive vehicles | Oct. 4, 1938 | 2,132,304 |
| Leonard, Herbert | Production of hydroxylamine hydrochloride | Jan. 28, 1964 | 3,119,657 |
| Leonard, Herbert | High impact polystyrene | June 22, 1971 | 3,586,740 |
| Leslie, Frank W. | Envelope seal | Sept. 21, 1897 | 590,325 |

# Dr. Raphael Lee's research offers fresh hope for people who suffer high-energy electrical burns

At the University of Chicago Medical Center where he is Director of the Electrical Trauma Program, Dr. Raphael Lee's research offers a new vision of hope for thousands of people who suffer high-energy electrical burns each year. Such burns, often from industrial accidents or lightning strikes, are far worse than ordinary thermal burns, which mainly affect surface areas. Electrical burns follow whatever path the current takes through the body. Of those victims who survive the initial shock, three-quarters lose a limb eventually, and almost all are permanently disabled. Dr. Lee, who was born in South Carolina in 1949, is one of those rare scientists who can move with

ease between the sciences. He has a doctorate in electrical engineering from the Massachusetts Institute of Technology as well as a MD. Dr. Lee felt strongly that the electrical field was the greater villain and not the heat generated by the body's electrical resistance. Dr. Lee believed that electroplated membranes damaged by heat could be resealed and salvaged. He turned to poloxamer 188, a soap like substance widely used as an emulsifier in drugs. P-188 worked in laboratory testing on rat tissue. If electroplated human membranes can be bathed in P-188 and healed in like fashion, there may be applications over and beyond electrical trauma.

# AFRICAN AMERICAN INVENTORS

| Inventor | Description of Invention | Date | Patent No. |
|---|---|---|---|
| LeVert, Francis Edward | Threshold self-powered gamma detector for use as a monitor of power in a nuclear reactor (LeVert has numerous patents in physics) | May 23, 1978 | 4,091,288 |
| LeVert, Francis Edward | Monitor for deposition on heat transfer surfaces | Feb. 2, 1988 | 4,722,610 |
| LeVert, Francis Edward | Continuous fluid level detector | Feb. 21, 1989 | 4,805,454 |
| Lewis, Anthony L. | Window cleaner | Sept. 27, 1892 | 483,359 |
| Lewis, Edward R. | Spring gun | May 3, 1887 | 362,096 |
| Lewis, James Earl | Antenna feed for two coordinate tracking radars | June 11, 1968 | 3,388,399 |
| Linden, Henry | Piano truck | Sept. 8, 1891 | 459,365 |
| Little, Ellis | Bridle-bit | March 7, 1882 | 254,666 |
| Logan, Emanuel L., Jr. | Door bar latch | July 13, 1971 | 3,592,497 |

# In 1994, Dr. Audrey F. Manley was named Deputy U.S. Surgeon General

Dr. Audrey F. Manley was named Deputy United States Surgeon General under Dr. Joycelyn Elders. A graduate of Meharry Medical College, Dr. Manley received her bachelors degree from Spelman College in Atlanta, Georgia. In January 1995, after Dr. Joycelyn Elders' resignation, Dr. Manley began serving as Acting United States. Surgeon General and the principal federal advisor to the nation on public health matters. In 1997, Dr. Manley was selected to become President of Spelman College, replacing Dr. Johnnetta Cole who retired in June 1997.

## AFRICAN AMERICAN INVENTORS

| Inventor | Description of Invention | Date | Patent No. |
|---|---|---|---|
| Long, Amos E. and Jones, Albert A. | Cap for bottle and jars | Sept. 13, 1898 | 610,715 |
| Loudin, Frederick J. | Fastener for the meeting rails of sashes | Dec. 12, 1893 | 510,432 |
| Loudin, Frederick J. | Key fastener | Jan. 9, 1894 | 512,308 |
| Love, John Lee | Plasterer's hawk | July 9, 1895 | 542,419 |
| Love, John Lee | Pencil sharpener | Nov. 23, 1897 | 594,114 |
| Lovell, Henry R. | Design for a doorcheck | Sept. 13, 1932 | D 87,753 |
| Lovett, William E. | Motor fuel composition | Sept. 18, 1962 | 3,054,666 |
| Lu Valle, James E. | Photographic processes | Nov. 23, 1965 | 3,219,445 |
| Lu Valle, James E. | Photographic medium and methods of preparing same | Nov. 23, 1965 | 3,219,448 |
| Lu Valle, James E. | Sensitizing photographic media | Nov. 23, 1965 | 3,219,451 |

# In 1919, Oscar Micheaux's motion picture, "Within Our Gates", was the first film produced and directed by an African American in the U. S.

Oscar Micheaux was born in Metropolis, IL. in 1884. Early in his life he worked as a Pullman porter, farmer, and rancher in South Dakota. He was a novelist and publisher before beginning the production of motion pictures. In 1919, he produced the silent motion picture, "Within Our Gates", a gritty portrayal of American race relations in the early 1900s. A black, southern woman, who is a schoolteacher, journeys north in search of money to keep her segregated school open. Her tale involves a lynching and she barely escapes being raped by a white man. Micheaux became the strongest black film producer in the 1920s. After "Gates" he produced "The Brute", "The Symbol Of The Unconquered", "Birthright", "The Conjure Woman", "The House Behind The Cedars", and "The Millionaire." Micheaux's style was an archly cynical mask that indicated racism, but his cinematic flair was hampered by a paucity of funds, a condition above, which he could never rise. This condition of being unable to obtain financing and preventing African American entrepreneurs from success continues to this day. Micheaux lapsed into bankruptcy at the end of the silent era and he died in 1951.

## AFRICAN AMERICAN INVENTORS

| Inventor | Description of Invention | Date | Patent No. |
|---|---|---|---|
| MacBeth, Arthur L. | Picture projection theater | June 13, 1922 | 1,419,281 |
| MacDonald, Hugh D., Jr. | Rocket catapult | June 3, 1969 | 3,447,767 |
| Mack, John L. | Participant-identification recording and playback system | June 17, 1986 | 4,596,041 |
| Madison, Shannon L. | Refrigerating apparatus | Sept. 28, 1965 | 3,208,232 |
| Madison, Shannon L. | Electrical wiring harness termination system | Dec. 27, 1988 | 4,793,820 |
| Madison, Walter G. | Flying machine | Dec. 10, 1912 | 1,047,098 |
| Maloney, Kenneth Morgan | Alumina coatings for an electric lamp | Feb. 25, 1975 | 3,868,266 |
| Maloney, Kenneth Morgan | Alumina coatings for mercury vapor lamps | March 14, 1978 | 4,079,288 |
| Mapp, Calvin R. | Disposable syringe | July 5, 1977 | 4,033,347 |
| Marshall, Willis | Grain binder | May 11, 1886 | 341,589 |

# In 1883, Jan Matzeliger revolutionized the shoe industry by inventing the Shoe Lasting Machine that increased the production and quality of shoes

Jan Ernest Matzeliger died when he was still a young man of 37. Yet, in his short lifetime he revolutionized the shoemaking industry. Born in Dutch Guiana of a Surinamese mother and a Dutch father in 1852, Matzeliger later worked in a shoe factory in Lynn, Massachusetts. He invented the Matzeliger Shoe Lasting Machine that both revolutionized the shoe industry and enabled the United Shoe Machinery Corporation, which had purchased his invention, to capture fully 98 percent of the shoe machinery trade. Matzeliger was among many 19th century black inventors who greatly influenced the lives of all Americans. The results of his invention were tremendous and the United States became the world leader in the shoe manufacturing industry. The leaders in shoe manufacturing worldwide could only produce 40 to 50 pair of shoes per day, by hand. Matzeliger's shoe lasting machine was able to produce thousands of pairs of shoes in a single day. His invention modernized the .shoe industry. Jan Matzeliger's portrait hangs in the First Church of Christ, the only congregation in Lynn, Massachusetts that welcomed him.

## AFRICAN AMERICAN INVENTORS

| Inventor | Description of Invention | Date | Patent No. |
|---|---|---|---|
| Martin, Thomas J. | Improvements in fire extinguishers | March 26, 1872 | 125,063 |
| Martin, Washington A. | Lock | July 23, 1889 | 407,738 |
| Martin, Washington A. | Lock | Dec. 30, 1890 | 443,945 |
| Mathis, Nathaniel | Barber's apron | Oct. 7, 1975 | D 237,022 |
| Matzeliger, Jan Earnst | Lasting machine (Matzeliger is credited for revolutionizing the U.S. shoe industry) | March 20, 1883 | 274,207 |
| Matzeliger, Jan Earnst | Nailing machine | Feb. 25, 1890 | 421,954 |
| Matzeliger, Jan Earnst | Tack separating and distributing mechanism | March 25, 1890 | 423,937 |
| Matzeliger, Jan Earnst | Lasting machine | Sept. 22, 1891 | 459,899 |
| Matzeliger, Jan Earnst | Mechanism for distributing tacks, nails, etc. | Nov. 26, 1899 | 415,726 |

| Inventor | Description of Invention | Date | Patent No. |
|---|---|---|---|
| McClennan, Walter N. | Automatic railway car door | March 9, 1920 | 1,333,430 |
| McClennan, Walter N. | Car door actuating mechanism | April 18, 1922 | RE 15,338 |
| McClennan, Walter N. | Coin mechanism | Dec. 9, 1924 | 1,518,208 |
| McCoy, Elijah | Improvement in lubricators for steam engines (McCoy received 25 patents for different types of lubricators between 1872 and 1899) | July 23, 1872 | 129,843 |
| McCoy, Elijah | Improvement in lubricators for steam engines | Aug. 6, 1872 | 130,305 |
| McCoy, Elijah | Improvement in lubricators | May 27, 1873 | 139,407 |
| McCoy, Elijah | Improvement in steam lubricators | Jan. 20, 1874 | 146,697 |
| McCoy, Elijah | Improvement in ironing tables | May 12, 1874 | 150,876 |
| McCoy, Elijah | Improvement in steam cylinder lubricator | Feb. 1, 1876 | 173,032 |

# Elijah McCoy's automatic lubricator for locomotives eliminated the risk of collisions between rolling trains and those stopped for oiling

When you hear the expression, "That's the real McCoy", you may wonder where it originated. Elijah McCoy was the son of runaway slaves. He was born in Canada, educated in Scotland and eventually settled in Detroit, Michigan. In 1872, he was granted a patent for an automatic oiling machine. This was very important to industry. Before McCoy's invention, workers had to constantly oil their machinery by hand which took a great deal of time and often shut down production entirely. McCoy's machine regulated the flow of oil to various parts of a mechanism and kept the machine running smoothly and efficiently. This machine also eliminated the risk of collisions between rolling trains and those stopped for oiling. Steam entered the device through the pipe at top, preventing the oil from congealing and forcing it out in regulated amounts to keep moving parts lubricated. Elijah McCoy proved to be one of the most prolific inventors in American history. He has invented devices from the ironing table to the lawn sprinkler. So the next time someone asks if something is the real McCoy, they are usually referring to something as important and special as the inventions of Elijah McCoy.

## AFRICAN AMERICAN INVENTORS

| Inventor | Description of Invention | Date | Patent No. |
|---|---|---|---|
| McCoy, Elijah | Improvement in steam cylinder lubricators | July 4, 1876 | 179,585 |
| McCoy, Elijah | Lubricator | March 28, 1882 | 255,443 |
| McCoy, Elijah | Lubricator | July 18, 1882 | 261,166 |
| McCoy, Elijah | Lubricator | Jan. 9, 1883 | 270,238 |
| McCoy, Elijah | Steam dome for locomotives | June 16, 1885 | 320,354 |
| McCoy, Elijah | Lubricator | June 16, 1885 | 320,379 |
| McCoy, Elijah | Lubricator | Feb. 8, 1887 | 357,491 |
| McCoy, Elijah | Lubricator attachment | April 19, 1887 | 361,435 |
| McCoy, Elijah | Lubricator for slide valves | May 24, 1887 | 363,529 |
| McCoy, Elijah | Lubricator | May 29, 1888 | 383,745 |

| Inventor | Description of Invention | Date | Patent No. |
|---|---|---|---|
| McCoy, Elijah | Lubricator | May 29, 1888 | 383,746 |
| McCoy, Elijah and Hodges, Clarence B. | Lubricator | Dec. 24, 1889 | 418,139 |
| McCoy, Elijah | Dope cup | Sept. 29, 1891 | 460,215 |
| McCoy, Elijah | Lubricator | Dec. 29, 1891 | 465,875 |
| McCoy, Elijah | Lubricator | March 1, 1892 | 470,163 |
| McCoy, Elijah | Lubricator | April 5, 1892 | 472,066 |
| McCoy, Elijah | Lubricator | June 6, 1893 | 498,809 |
| McCoy, Elijah | Lubricator | Sept. 13, 1898 | 610,634 |
| McCoy, Elijah | Lubricator | Oct. 4, 1898 | 611,759 |
| McCoy, Elijah | Oil cup | Nov. 15, 1898 | 614,307 |

| Inventor | Description of Invention | Date | Patent No. |
|---|---|---|---|
| McCoy, Elijah | Lubricator | June 27, 1899 | 627,623 |
| McCoy, Melvin | Multi-purpose uniaxial litter enginery or M.U.L.E. | May 12, 1987 | 4,664,395 |
| McCree, Daniel | Portable fire escape | Nov. 11, 1890 | 440,322 |
| McGee, Hansel L. | Method of preparation of carbon transfer inks | Oct. 26, 1965 | 3,214,282 |
| McNair, Luther | Sanitary attachment for drinking glasses | Aug. 6, 1912 | 1,034,636 |
| Mendenhall, Albert | Holder for driving reins | Nov. 28, 1899 | 637,811 |
| Miles, Alexander | Elevator | Oct. 11, 1887 | 371,207 |
| Millington, James E. | Thermostable dielectric material | April 25, 1967 | 3,316,178 |
| Millington, James E. | Method of making expandable styrene-type beads | Aug. 25, 1981 | 4,286,069 |
| Millington, James E. | Method of making styrene-type polymer | March 8, 1988 | 4,730,027 |

| Inventor | Description of Invention | Date | Patent No. |
|---|---|---|---|
| Mitchell, Charles Lewis | Device for aid in vocal culture | Jan. 1, 1884 | 291,071 |
| Mitchell, James M. | Check row corn planter | Jan. 16, 1900 | 641,462 |
| Mitchell, James W. | Method for growing continuous diamond films | Aug. 15, 1995 | 5,441,013 |
| Montgomery, Jay H. and Burton, Edward F. | Food product and process of producing the same ( compound of honey and butter ) | Dec. 11, 1928 | 1,694,680 |
| Montgomery, Jay H. | Aeroplane aerofoil wing | May 23, 1933 | 1,910,626 |
| Moody, William U. | Design for a game board | May 11, 1897 | D 27,046 |
| Moore, Samuel | Self-directing headlight | Nov. 30, 1926 | 1,608,903 |
| Moore, Samuel | Vehicle- headlight mechanism | Feb. 7, 1928 | 1,658,534 |
| Moore, Samuel | Locomotive headlight | Feb. 14, 1928 | 1,659,328 |
| Moore, Samuel | Hobby horse | March 19, 1929 | 1,705,991 |

# Garrett Morgan's Breathing Hood (gas mask) and Traffic Signal inventions made him a life saving inventor all over the world

In 1912, Garrett Morgan invented a "breathing device", which was an early version of the gas mask. Morgan's device was a natural for fire and police departments. He himself gave it a dramatic real-life test. On July 24, 1916, a tunnel explosion five miles out into Lake Erie and 250 feet below the surface, had trapped 11 workers. Ten rescuers went down into the dangerous atmosphere of toxic fumes, smoke and dust. All ten rescuers were killed. Then Garrett Morgan, his brother, Frank, and two other volunteers wearing Morgan's hoods with long breathing tubes, descended into the deathtrap and managed to bring out two survivors and four bodies. Newspapers around the world reported the valiant rescue and orders for the hood flooded in. But when buyers learned that Morgan was black, many canceled. Morgan was awarded a gold medal at the 2nd International Exposition of Safety and Sanitation in New York City and a gold medal from the City of Cleveland. Later, while driving in Cleveland, Morgan saw a car collide with a horse and carriage. The incident inspired him in 1923 to invent a signal for managing traffic at intersections. Morgan sold the patent rights to the device, which ultimately became the traffic light, to General Electric for $40,000. A small amount for an invention that would also save millions of lives in the future. Garrett Morgan's inventions continue to save lives to this day. He died in 1963.

## AFRICAN AMERICAN INVENTORS

| Inventor | Description of Invention | Date | Patent No. |
|---|---|---|---|
| Moore, Samuel | Fuel-valve lock for motor vehicles | June 25, 1935 | 2,006,027 |
| Morehead, King | Reel carrier | Oct. 6, 1896 | 568,916 |
| Morgan, Garrett Augustus | Breathing device (Morgan used this device in 1916 to save workers trapped in a tunnel) | Oct. 13, 1914 | 1,113,675 |
| Morgan, Garrett Augustus | Traffic signal ( Morgan created the forerunner of modern traffic lights) | Nov. 20, 1923 | 1,475,024 |
| Morris, Joel Morton | Switching system charging arrangement | Aug. 29, 1972 | 3,688,047 |
| Muckelroy, William L. | Leadless microminiature inductance element with closed magnetic circuit | Sept. 21, 1972 | 3,691,497 |
| Muckelroy, William L. | Ceramic inductor | May 21, 1974 | 3,812,442 |
| Mullen, Nathaniel John | Asphalt paving vehicles | April 29, 1975 | 3,880,542 |

| Inventor | Description of Invention | Date | Patent No. |
|----------|-------------------------|------|------------|
| Murdock, Wilbert | Knee alignment monitoring apparatus | Sept. 2, 1986 | 4,608,998 |
| Murray, George W. | Combined furrow opener and stalk-knocker | April 10, 1894 | 517,960 |
| Murray, George W. | Cultivator and marker | April 10, 1894 | 517,961 |
| Murray, George W. | Planter | June 5, 1894 | 520,887 |
| Murray, George W. | Cotton chopper | June 5, 1894 | 520,888 |
| Murray, George W. | Fertilizer distributor | June 5, 1894 | 520,889 |
| Murray, George W. | Planter | June 5, 1894 | 520,890 |
| Murray, George W. | Combined cotton seed planter and fertilizer distributor | June 5, 1894 | 520,891 |
| Murray, George W. | Reaper | June 5, 1894 | 520,892 |
| Murray, William | Corn harvester | Feb. 1, 1870 | 99,463 |

# The Patterson-Greenfield Automobile

**Special Features:** ▪ **Full floating rear axle** ▪ **Cantilever spring**
▪ **Electric starting and lighting system**

**Special motor has that surplus power**

**Ventilating Windshield**

**Demountable rims**

**Left hand drive**

**Four Door Touring Car**

# Frederick Douglas Patterson became one of America's first black automobile manufacturers when his car rolled off the line on Sept. 23, 1915

Frederick D. Patterson attributed the manufacturing of his car in 1915, to his father, Charles "Rich" Patterson. One of the wealthiest men in his hometown of Greenfield, Ohio, Patterson was the owner of the C.R. Patterson and Sons Carriage Company of Greenfield. An ex-slave, Charles Patterson had fled from slavery just before the Civil War in 1861. He eventually made it to Greenfield, Ohio, which was an important link along the Underground Railroad. Patterson immediately got a job at the Dines and Simpson Carriage and Coach Makers Company where he later became a partner. He married and had four children. Charles eventually brought out his white partner and became sole owner. His son, Frederick became the first black to play on Ohio State University's football team. When he returned to Greenfield he joined the family's carriage business. Shortly there after, his father died, leaving Frederick to operate the company. In search of more business, Frederick decided to build a horseless carriage. His plan was bold. He wanted to build a vehicle that could compete against any car on the market. On Sept. 23, 1915 he saw his dream role off the line. Word about the new vehicle swept across the state and it was considered to have better bodywork than horseless carriages being manufactured in Detroit by some man named Henry Ford. However, the Patterson dream of manufacturing automobiles was stopped short due to lack of capital and slow sales. Frederick was forced to turn his attention to producing school bus bodies, which were in great demand at that time in rural America.

# AFRICAN AMERICAN INVENTORS

| Inventor | Description of Invention | Date | Patent No. |
|---|---|---|---|
| Murray, William | Attachment for bicycles | Jan. 27, 1891 | 445,452 |
| Nance, Lee | Game apparatus | Dec. 1, 1891 | 464,035 |
| Nash, Henry H. | Improvement in life-preserving stools | Oct. 5, 1875 | 168,519 |
| Nauflett, George W. | Process for the synthesis of 2- flouro-2, 2- dinitroethanol | March 28, 1972 | 3,652,686 |
| Neal, Lonnie G. | Electromagnetic gyroscope float assembly | Nov. 4, 1969 | 3,475,975 |
| Neal, Theophilus Ealey | Automatic blow-off | Nov. 1, 1932 | 1,885,466 |
| Neal, Theophilus Ealey | Shower bath spray | Jan. 3, 1933 | 1,893,435 |
| Neblett, Richard Flemon | Gasoline composition | Oct. 11, 1960 | 2,955,928 |
| Neblett, Richard Flemon | Motor fuel composition | Sept. 18, 1962 | 3,054,666 |

| Inventor | Description of Invention | Date | Patent No. |
|---|---|---|---|
| Neblett, Richard Flemon | Oil-soluble ashless disperant-detergent-inhibitors | May 12, 1970 | 3,511,780 |
| Newman, Lyda D. | Brush | Nov. 15, 1898 | 614,335 |
| Newson, Simeon | Oil heater or cooker | May 22, 1894 | 520,188 |
| Nickerson, William J. | Mandolin and guitar attachment for pianos | June 27, 1899 | 627,739 |
| Nokes, Clarence | Venetian blind restringer | June 3, 1958 | 2,836,882 |
| Nokes, Clarence | Lawn mower | Feb. 12, 1963 | 3,077,066 |
| O'Connor, John and Turner, Collatinus A. | Alarm for boilers | Aug. 25, 1896 | 566,612 |
| O'Connor, John and Turner, Collatinus A. | Steam gage | Aug. 25, 1896 | 566,613 |
| O'Connor, John and Turner, Collatinus A. | Alarm for water containing vessels | Feb. 8, 1898 | 598,572 |
| Outlaw, John W. | Horseshoe | Nov. 15, 1898 | 614,273 |

# Gordon Parks is an African American artist who faced adversity in the form of racism and maintained his uncommon and uncompromising vision to become successful

Gordon Parks is a renowned photographer with an uncommon and uncompromising vision. He has won a Rosenwald Fellowship and a TV Emmy Award. Parks worked as a staff photographer for both Time and Life Magazines. In addition, he is a painter, novelist, composer and he has produced and directed a series of major motion pictures and documentaries including *The Learning Tree, Shaft, Shaft's Big Score* and *Leadbelly.* Parks has equally been successful in the highly competitive worlds of high fashion and celebrity photography. With the world as his neighborhood for more than a half century, Gordon Parks has powerfully chronicled humanity and its many struggles throughout the world. He has displayed the dignity and squalor of life in the inner-city tenements and the indignity of *Colored Only* water fountains in the Jim Crow south. In the year 1998, when he was 84, Parks was honored with an extensive art exhibition tour of his works entitled, *Half Past Autumn: The Art of Gordon Parks.* This art exhibition was proudly received in cities across the country.

## AFRICAN AMERICAN INVENTORS

| Inventor | Description of Invention | Date | Patent No. |
| --- | --- | --- | --- |
| Page, Lionel F. | Auxiliary circulating device for automobile heaters | Aug. 22, 1939 | 2,170,032 |
| Parker, Alice H. | Heating furnace | Dec. 23, 1919 | 1,325,905 |
| Parker, John Percial | Follower-screw for tobacco presses | Sept. 2, 1884 | 304,552 |
| Parker, John Percial | Portable screw press | May 19, 1885 | 318,285 |
| Parsons, James A., Jr. | Iron alloy | Sept. 17, 1929 | 1,728,360 |
| Parsons, James A., Jr. | Method of making silicon iron | Aug. 18, 1931 | 1,819,479 |
| Parsons, James A., Jr. | Process for treating silicon alloy castings | Sept. 4, 1934 | 1,972,103 |
| Parsons, James A., Jr. | Corrosion-resisting ferrous alloy | May 7, 1940 | 2,200,208 |
| Payne, Moses | Horseshoe | Dec. 11, 1888 | 394,388 |
| Pelham, Robert A. | Pasting apparatus | Dec. 19, 1905 | 807,685 |

# Dr. Hildrus Poindexter became an expert on tropical diseases during World War II and continued with health service all over the world after the war

Dr. Hildrus Poindexter was a researcher and physician who was born into poverty in 1901. He became one of U.S. Department of Health's most important medical researchers. After attending medical school at Dartmouth and Harvard, he eventually joined the Public Health Service. Soon after, the world was thrown into chaos as World War II erupted. Poindexter was stationed in the tropics and became an expert on diseases peculiar to that region. After the war, Dr. Poindexter continued with his Health Service and went wherever his expertise was needed. Africa, Latin America, and Southeast Asia all benefited from his extensive knowledge of tropical disease. Hildrus "Gus" Poindexter never forgot that being a professional means sharing your knowledge with others. He spent the last years of his life at Howard University, training young people who would follow in his footsteps. He died in 1979.

## AFRICAN AMERICAN INVENTORS

| Inventor | Description of Invention | Date | Patent No. |
|---|---|---|---|
| Perry, John Jr. and Hunger, Herbert F. | Biochemical fuel cell | Nov. 8, 1966 | 3,284,239 |
| Perryman, Frank R. | Caterers- tray table | Feb. 2, 1892 | 468,038 |
| Peterson, Charles A. | Power generating apparatus | July 9, 1968 | 3,391,903 |
| Peterson, Henry | Attachment for lawn mowers | April 30, 1889 | 402,189 |
| Phelps, William Henry | Apparatus for washing vehicles | March 23, 1897 | 579,242 |
| Pickering, John F. | Air ship (Blimp) | Feb. 20, 1900 | 643,975 |
| Pickett, Henry | Improvement in scaffolds | June 30, 1874 | 152,511 |
| Pinn, Traverse B. | File holder | Aug. 17, 1880 | 231,355 |
| Polite, William D. | Gun | March 6, 1917 | 1,218,458 |
| Polk, Austin J. | Bicycle support | April 14, 1896 | 558,103 |

| Inventor | Description of Invention | Date | Patent No. |
|---|---|---|---|
| Pope, Jessie T. | Croquignole iron | Oct. 22, 1946 | 2,409,791 |
| Porter, James Hall | Gas well sulphur removal by diffusion through polymeric membranes | Oct. 20, 1970 | 3,534,528 |
| Prather, Alfred G. B. | Gravity escape means | Feb. 6, 1973 | 3,715,011 |
| Prince, Frank Rodger | Production of 2-pyrrolidones | Jan. 25, 1972 | 3,637,743 |
| Pugsley, Abraham | Blind stop | July 29, 1890 | 433,306 |
| Pugsley, Abraham | Shutter worker | Aug. 5, 1890 | 433,819 |
| Pugsley, Samuel | Gate latch | Feb. 15, 1887 | 357,787 |
| Purdy, John E. and Sadgwar, Daniel A. | Folding chair | June 11, 1889 | 405, 117 |
| Purdy, Walter | Device for sharpening edged tools | Oct. 27, 1896 | 570,337 |
| Purdy, Walter | Device for sharpening edged tools | Aug. 16, 1898 | 609,367 |

| Inventor | Description of Invention | Date | Patent No. |
|---|---|---|---|
| Purdy, Walter | Device for sharpening edged tools | Aug. 1, 1899 | 630,106 |
| Purdy, William H. and Peters, Leonard C. | Design for a spoon | April 23, 1895 | D 24,228 |
| Purvis, William B. | Bag fastener | April 25, 1882 | 256,856 |
| Purvis, William B. | Hand stamp | Feb. 27, 1883 | 273,149 |
| Purvis, William B. | Paper bag machine | Feb. 12, 1884 | 293,353 |
| Purvis, William B. | Fountain pen | Jan. 7, 1890 | 419,065 |
| Purvis, William B. | Paper bag machine | Jan. 28, 1890 | 420,099 |
| Purvis, William B. | Electric railway | May 1, 1894 | 519,291 |
| Purvis, William B. | Magnetic car balancing device | May 21, 1895 | 539,542 |
| Purvis, William B. | Electrical railway system | Aug. 17, 1897 | 588,176 |

| Inventor | Description of Invention | Date | Patent No. |
|----------|-------------------------|------|------------|
| Queen, William | Guard for companion ways or hatches | Aug. 18, 1891 | 458,131 |
| Ransom, Victor Llewellyn | Traffic data processing system | Jan. 25, 1966 | 3,231,866 |
| Ransom, Victor Llewellyn | Method and apparatus for gathering peak load traffic data | Feb. 11, 1975 | 3,866,185 |
| Ratchford, Debrilla M. | Suitcase with wheels and transporting hook | June 13, 1978 | 4,094,391 |
| Ray, Ernest P. | Chair supporting device | Feb. 21, 1899 | 620,078 |
| Ray, Lloyd P. | Dust pan | Aug. 3, 1897 | 587,607 |
| Reed, Judy W. | Dough kneader and roller | Sept. 23, 1884 | 305, 474 |
| Reynolds, Humphrey H. | Window ventilator for railway cars | April 3, 1883 | 275, 271 |
| Reynolds, Humphrey H. | Safety gate for bridges | Oct. 7, 1890 | 437,937 |
| Reynolds, Mary Jane | Hoisting and loading mechanism | April 20, 1920 | 1,337,667 |

| Inventor | Description of Invention | Date | Patent No. |
| --- | --- | --- | --- |
| Reynolds, Robert Randolph | Nonrefillable bottle | May 2, 1899 | 624,092 |
| Rhodes, Jerome Bonaparte | Water closet | Dec. 19, 1899 | 639,290 |
| Richardson, Albert C. | Ham fastener | March 14, 1882 | 255,022 |
| Richardson, Albert C. | Churn | Feb. 17, 1891 | 446,470 |
| Richardson, Albert C. | Casket- lowering device | Nov. 13, 1894 | 529,311 |
| Richardson, Albert C. | Insect destroyer | Feb. 28, 1899 | 620,362 |
| Richardson, Albert C. | Bottle | Dec. 12, 1899 | 638,811 |
| Richardson, William H. | Cotton chopper | June 1, 1886 | 343,140 |
| Richardson, William H. | Child's carriage | June 18, 1889 | 405,599 |
| Richardson, William H. | Child's carriage | June 18, 1889 | 405,600 |

| Inventor | Description of Invention | Date | Patent No. |
|---|---|---|---|
| Richey, Charles V. | Car coupling | June 15, 1897 | 584,650 |
| Richey, Charles V. | Railroad switch | Aug. 3, 1897 | 587,657 |
| Richey, Charles V. | Railroad switch | Oct. 26, 1897 | 592,448 |
| Richey, Charles V. | Fire escape bracket | Dec. 28, 1897 | 596,427 |
| Richey, Charles V. | Combined cot, hammock and stretcher | Dec. 13, 1898 | 615,907 |
| Richey, Charles V. | Telephone register and lock-out device | June 3, 1913 | 1,063,599 |
| Richey, Charles V. | Lockout for outgoing calls for telephone systems | July 7, 1931 | 1,812,984 |
| Richey, Charles V. | Time control system for telephones | Feb. 14, 1933 | 1,897,533 |
| Rickman, Alvin Longo | Overshoe | Feb. 8, 1898 | 598,816 |
| Ricks, James | Horseshoe | March 30, 1886 | 338,781 |

# Norbert Rillieux was a mechanical engineer who revolutionized the sugar industry when he patented a sugar refining process in 1864

The son of a slave mother and the master of the plantation where he was born in New Orleans, Louisiana in 1806, Norbert Rillieux always possessed a sharp mind and an eagerness to learn. By his father being a successful engineer who recognized the child's ability, he was sent to Paris to study where he became fascinated with the field of mechanical engineering. By the time he was 24 years old, he was an instructor at L'ecole Centrale (Central School) in Paris, but it was after his return to his native New Orleans that he made his most significant contributions. Observing that the methods used for refining sugar were crude and dangerous, requiring back-breaking labor, he set about to develop a method that would be safer and would refine sugar into the small granules we are

familiar with today. The process he developed greatly reduced the cost of producing good sugar from sugar cane and from sugar beet. The invention increased sugar production and reduced operating costs for the plantation system. Soon, his method was being used worldwide and he was named responsible for the sugar refining industry of Cuba. These methods are still being used today and have been adapted for soap, gelatin, glue and many other products that require refining. He also published papers on the uses of steam and on the steam engine. In 1854, because of racial discrimination in Louisiana, he left that state for good, returning to France where he again turned to engineering inventions. Rillieux died in 1894.

## AFRICAN AMERICAN INVENTORS

| Inventor | Description of Invention | Date | Patent No. |
|---|---|---|---|
| Ricks, James | Overshoe for horses | June 6, 1899 | 626,245 |
| Rillieux, Norbert | Improvement in sugar works (Rillieux's inventions completely changed the sugar industry) | Aug. 26, 1843 | 3,237 |
| Rillieux, Norbert | Improvement in sugar making (evaporating pan) | Dec. 10, 1846 | 4,879 |
| Roberts, Louis W. | Gaseous discharge device | Jan. 8, 1963 | 3,072,865 |
| Roberts, Louis W. | GASAR (Device for gas amplication by stimulated emission and radiation) | June 21, 1966 | 3,257,620 |
| Roberts, Louis W. | Gallium-wetted movable electrode switch | April 9, 1968 | 3,377,576 |
| Robinson, Elbert R. | Electric railway trolley | Sept. 19, 1893 | 505,370 |
| Robinson, Elbert R. | Casting composite or other car wheels | Nov. 23, 1897 | 594,286 |

| Inventor | Description of Invention | Date | Patent No. |
|---|---|---|---|
| Robinson, Hassel D. | Design for a traffic signal casing | Feb, 24, 1925 | D 66,703 |
| Robinson, Hassel D. | Traffic signal for automobiles | April 13, 1926 | 1,580,218 |
| Robinson, Ira C. | Sustained release pharmaceutical tablets | May 4, 1971 | 3,577,514 |
| Robinson, James H. | Lifesaving guard for locomotives | March 14, 1899 | 621,143 |
| Robinson, James H. | Lifesaving guard for street cars | April 25, 1899 | 623,929 |
| Robinson, John | Dinner pail | Feb. 1, 1887 | 356,852 |
| Robinson, Neal Moore | Vehicle wheel | July 11, 1922 | 1,422,479 |
| Romain, Arnold | Passenger register | April 23, 1889 | 402,035 |
| Rose, Raymond E. | Control apparatus | Nov. 9, 1971 | 3,618,388 |
| Ross, Archia L. | Runner for stoops | Aug. 4, 1896 | 565,301 |

# Dr. Louis Roberts has contributed to the development of using electricity, natural gas and other fuel sources to drive automobiles

Dr. Louis W. Roberts was an energy conservationist who was born in 1913. Roberts was the head of the Department of Transportation Systems Center in Cambridge, Mass. As part of this research, Dr. Roberts worked on developing energy-saving transportation. Dr. Roberts received much of his education at Fisk University and the University of Michigan. He was considered an expert in the fields of mathematics, physics, and electronics. He was especially interested in the field of optics and microwave research. He once headed NASA's Electronic Research Center and operated his own research company. He has served in the departments of mathematics and physics at Howard University and St. Augustine College. Dr. Roberts has also written many papers on electromagnetism, optics, and microwaves. Roberts' creativity has earned him 11 patents, all for electronic devices. The day will come when we will be able to drive cars using electricity, natural gas, or other fuel sources. When that happens, we should thank Dr. Louis Roberts for his many contributions to this development. Roberts died in 1995.

## AFRICAN AMERICAN INVENTORS

| Inventor | Description of Invention | Date | Patent No. |
|---|---|---|---|
| Ross, Archia L. | Bag closure | June 7, 1898 | 605,343 |
| Ross, Archia L. | Trousers support or stretcher | Nov. 28, 1899 | 638,068 |
| Ross, Joseph | Hay press | Sept. 5, 1899 | 632,539 |
| Roston, David N. | Feather curler | March 10, 1896 | 556,166 |
| Russell, Edwin R. | The separation of plutonium from uranium and fission products | Oct. 7, 1958 | 2,855,269 |
| Russell, Edwin R. | Ion exchange adsorption process for plutonium separation | July 11, 1961 | 2,992,249 |
| Russell, Edwin R. | Removal of cesium from aqueous solution by ion exchange | Jan. 3, 1967 | 3,296,123 |
| Russell, Edwin R. | Thorium oxide or thorium-uranium oxide with magnesium oxide | March 14, 1967 | 3,309,323 |
| Russell, Jesse Eugene | Broadband data reception system for Worldnet access | July 27, 1999 | 5,930,247 |

# In February 1998, Dr. David Satcher became the 16<sup>th</sup> Surgeon General of the United States and the third African American to be appointed

Born in Anniston, Alabama, on March 2, 1941, Dr. David Satcher graduated from Morehouse College in Atlanta in 1963 and was elected to Phi Beta Kappa. He received his M.D. and Ph.D. from Case Western Reserve University in 1970 with election to Alpha Omega Alpha Honor Society. Dr. Satcher served simultaneously in the positions of United States Surgeon General and Assistant Secretary of Health from February 1998 through January 2001. He also held the posts of Director of the Center For Disease Control and Prevention and Administrator of the Agency for Toxic Substances and Disease Registry from 1993 to 1998. Before joining the administration, he was President of Meharry Medical College in Nashville from 1982 to 1993. Dr. Satcher and his wife, Nola, reside in Bethesda, Maryland and have four grown children.

## AFRICAN AMERICAN INVENTORS

| Inventor | Description of Invention | Date | Patent No. |
|---|---|---|---|
| Russell, Jesse Eugene | Network server platform for Internet, Java server and video application server | March 28, 2000 | 6,044,403 |
| Russell, Joseph L. | Preparation of tungsten hexafluoride from halogen and hydrogen fluoride | Nov. 30, 1976 | 3,995,011 |
| Russell, Lewis A. | Guard attachment for beds | Aug. 13, 1895 | 544,381 |
| Ryder, Earl | High silicon cast iron | April 14, 1964 | 3,129,095 |
| Sammons, Walter H. | Comb | Dec. 21, 1920 | 1,362,823 |
| Samms, Adolphus | Rocket engine pump feed system | Sept. 19, 1961 | 3,000,179 |
| Samms, Adolphus | Multiple stage rocket | Aug. 10, 1965 | 3,199,455 |
| Samms, Adolphus | Emergency release for extraction chute | June 21, 1966 | 3,257,089 |
| Samms, Adolphus | Rocket motor fuel feed | March 28, 1967 | 3,310,938 |

| Inventor | Description of Invention | Date | Patent No. |
|----------|-------------------------|------|------------|
| Sampson, George T. | Sled propeller | Feb. 17, 1885 | 312,388 |
| Sampson, George T. | Clothes drier | June 7, 1892 | 476,416 |
| Sampson, Henry Thomas | Binder system for propellants and explosives | July 7, 1964 | 3,140,210 |
| Sampson, Henry Thomas | Case bonding system for cast composite propellants | Oct. 19, 1965 | 3,212,256 |
| Sampson, Henry Thomas | Gamma electric cell (cellular phone) | July 6, 1971 | 3,591,860 |
| Sanderson, Dewey S.C. | Urinalysis machine | July 28, 1970 | 3,522,011 |
| Sanderson, Ralph W. | Hydraulic shock absorber | Jan. 9, 1968 | 3,362,742 |
| Saxton, Richard L. | Pay telephone with sanitized tissue dispenser | July 5, 1983 | 4,392,028 |
| Scharschmidt, Virginia | Safety window cleaning device | April 9, 1929 | 1,708,594 |

| Inventor | Description of Invention | Date | Patent No. |
|---|---|---|---|
| Scott, Henry | Spinal traction and support unit used while seated | Nov. 21, 1989 | 4,881,528 |
| Scott, Howard L. | Treating human, animal and synthetic hair with a waterproofing composition | March 9, 1971 | 3,568,685 |
| Scott, J. C. | Shadow box | Oct. 1, 1968 | D 212,334 |
| Scott, Linzy | Knee brace | June 30, 1981 | 4,275,716 |
| Scott, Robert P. | Corn silker | Aug. 7, 1894 | 524,223 |
| Scottron, Samuel R. | Adjustable window cornice | Feb. 17, 1880 | 224,732 |
| Scottron, Samuel R. | Cornice | Jan. 16, 1883 | 270,851 |
| Scottron, Samuel R. | Pole tip | Sept. 21, 1886 | 349,525 |
| Scottron, Samuel R. | Curtain rod | Aug. 30, 1892 | 481,720 |
| Scottron, Samuel R. | Supporting bracket | Sept. 12, 1893 | 505,008 |

| Inventor | Description of Invention | Date | Patent No. |
|---|---|---|---|
| Shaw, Earl D. | Free-electron amplifier device with electromagnetic radiation delay element | July 16, 1985 | 4,529,942 |
| Shorter, Dennis W. | Feed rack | May 17, 1887 | 363,089 |
| Sigur, Wanda A. | Method of fabricating composite structures | Jan. 28, 1992 | 5,084,219 |
| Silvera, Esteban | Ram-valve level indicator | Feb. 27, 1973 | 3,718,157 |
| Skanks, Stephen Chambers | Sleeping car berth register | July 27, 1897 | 587,165 |
| Small, Isadore | Universal on-delay timer | June 4, 1974 | 3,814,948 |
| Smartt, Brinay | Reversing-valve | Sept. 12, 1905 | 799,498 |
| Smartt, Brinay | Valve gear | Sept. 28, 1909 | 935,169 |
| Smartt, Brinay | Wheel | Feb. 14, 1913 | 1,052,290 |

| Inventor | Description of Invention | Date | Patent No. |
|---|---|---|---|
| Smith, Bernard | Method or preparing nonlaminating anisotropic boron nitride | Oct. 1, 1985 | 4,544,535 |
| Smith, John Winsor | Game | April 17, 1900 | 647,887 |
| Smith, Johnathan S. | Transparent zirconia composition and process for making same | March 11, 1969 | 3,432,314 |
| Smith, Joseph H. | Lawn sprinkler | May 4, 1897 | 581,785 |
| Smith, Joseph H. | Lawn sprinkler | March 22, 1898 | 601,065 |
| Smith, Mildred E. | Family relationships card game | Oct. 28, 1980 | 4,230,321 |
| Smith, Morris L. | Printing fluid comprising an aqueous solution of a water-soluble dye and a thermosetting vinylsulfonium polymer | June 18, 1968 | 3,389,108 |
| Smith, Morris L. | Chemically treated paper products-towel and tissue | Nov. 21, 1989 | 4,882,221 |

# Two African American professors, Michael Spencer and Gary Harris, spearhead Howard University's research into Microelectronics

Both Michael Spencer (standing) and Gary Harris are Cornell graduates of 1980. They were the first African Americans ever to receive electrical engineering doctorates from Cornell. Today, with their home base at Howard University's Materials Science Research Center, they have become the pacesetters in microelectronics by working with dazzling new materials and mechanisms to extend the performance of everything from satellite communications systems and supercomputers to lasers and jet engines. Spencer and Harris are well aware of their special role at Howard and of Howard University's special role in the black community. The two professors are dedicated teachers as well and are committed and determine to successfully train African American engineers. To insure a steady flow of students, the two have recruited masters and doctoral candidates from a number of black colleges. The National Science Foundation, the National Aeronautics Space Program (NASA), and private sources have funded them in the past.

# AFRICAN AMERICAN INVENTORS

| Inventor | Description of Invention | Date | Patent No. |
|---|---|---|---|
| Smith, Morris L. | Chemically treated paper products- towel and tissue | Nov. 28, 1989 | 4,883,475 |
| Smith, Peter D. | Potato digger | Jan. 27, 1891 | 445,206 |
| Smith, Peter D. | Grain binder | Feb. 23, 1892 | 469,279 |
| Smith, Robert T. | Spraying machine | Aug. 21,1934 | 1,970,984 |
| Smith, Samuel C. | Hardness tester | May 18, 1976 | 3,956,925 |
| Smoot, Lanny S. | Optical receiver circuit with active equalizer | Jan. 21, 1986 | 4,565,974 |
| Smoot, Lanny S. | Teleconferencing facility with high resolution video display | Dec. 26, 1989 | 4,890,314 |
| Smoot, Lanny S. | Teleconferencing terminal with camera behind display screen | May 22, 1990 | 4,928,301 |
| Snow, William and Johns, James A. | Liniment | Oct. 7, 1890 | 437,728 |

| Inventor | Description of Invention | Date | Patent No. |
|---|---|---|---|
| Spears, Harde | Improvement in portable shields infantry and artillery | Dec. 27, 1870 | 110,599 |
| Spikes, Richard B. | Billiard rack | Oct. 11,1910 | 972,277 |
| Spikes, Richard Bowie | Combination milk bottle opener and cover | June 29, 1926 | 1,590,557 |
| Spikes, Richard B. | Method and apparatus for obtaining average samples and temperature of tank liquids | Oct. 27, 1931 | 1,828,753 |
| Spikes, Richard B. | Automatic gear shift | Dec. 6, 1932 | 1,889,814 |
| Spikes, Richard B. | Transmission and shifting means therefore | Nov. 28, 1933 | 1,936,996 |
| Spikes, Richard B. | Automatic safety brake system | Jan. 2, 1962 | 3,015,522 |
| Stafford, Osbourne C. | Microwave phase shift device | Aug. 4, 1970 | 3,522,558 |
| Stallworth, Elbert | Electric heater | .Oct. 16, 1928 | 1,687,521 |

| Inventor | Description of Invention | Date | Patent No. |
|---|---|---|---|
| Stallworth, Elbert | Electric chamber | Sept. 10, 1929 | 1,727,842 |
| Stallworth, Elbert | Alarm clock electric switch | Sept. 4, 1934 | 1,972,634 |
| Standard, John | Oil stove | Oct. 29, 1889 | 413,689 |
| Standard, John | Refrigerator | July 14, 1891 | 455,891 |
| Stancell, Arnold F. | Separating fluids with selective membranes | April 18, 1972 | 3,657,113 |
| Stephens, George B. D. | Cigarette holder and ash tray | Sept. 11, 1956 | 2,762,377 |
| Stewart, Thomas | Metal bending machine | Dec. 27, 1887 | 375,512 |
| Stewart, Albert Clifton | Redox couple radiation cell | June 7, 1966 | 3,255,044 |
| Stewart, Albert Clifton | Electric cell | June 7, 1966 | 3,255,045 |
| Stewart, Earl M. and Shagrin, Seymour | Arch and heel support | Feb. 18, 1936 | 2,031,510 |

| Inventor | Description of Invention | Date | Patent No. |
|----------|------------------------|------|------------|
| Stewart, Enos W. | Punching machine | May 3, 1887 | 362,190 |
| Stewart, Enos W. | Machine for forming vehicle seat bars | Nov. 22, 1887 | 373,698 |
| Stewart, Marvin Charles | Arithmetic unit for digital computers | July 30, 1968 | 3,395,271 |
| Stewart, Marvin Charles | System for interconnecting electrical components | Sept. 14, 1971 | 3,605,063 |
| Stewart, Thomas W. | Mop | June 13, 1893 | 499,402 |
| Stewart, Thomas W. | Station indicator | June 20, 1893 | 499,895 |
| Stilwell, Henry F. | Means for receiving mail and other matter on aeroplanes while in motion | May 30, 1933 | 1,911,248 |
| Stokes, Rufus | Exhaust purifier | April 16, 1968 | 3,378,241 |
| Stokes, Rufus | Air pollution control device | July 14, 1970 | 3,520,113 |

# Rufus Stokes' invention for air purification allows people worldwide to breathe easier and enables industries to clean up their environments

Rufus Stokes was born in Alabama in 1924. At an early age he realized that clean air is needed to survive by every living creature on the Earth. He became one of the leading innovators in the fight when he worked as a machinist for an incinerator company in Illinois. He was able to study first hand, the problems of cleaning the air that is expelled from the incinerators. In 1968 he received a U.S. Patent for an air purification device that reduces the level of gases and ash emissions from furnace and power plant smokestacks. This invention was so successful that it is able to make the smoke nearly invisible. Stokes tested and demonstrated several models of stack filters, termed the "clean air machine", in Chicago and elsewhere to show its versatility. The system benefited the respiratory health of people and eased the health risks to plants and animals. A side effect of reduced industrial smokestack emissions was the improved appearance and durability of buildings, cars, and objects exposed to outdoor pollution for lengthy periods. There are several adaptations of Stokes' purification system presently in use, which enable many industries to clean up their environments. Millions of people all over the world will be able to breath easier once the system developed by Rufus Stokes is in massive and full implementation. He died in 1986.

# AFRICAN AMERICAN INVENTORS

| Inventor | Description of Invention | Date | Patent No. |
|---|---|---|---|
| Sutton, Edward H. | Improvement in cotton cultivators | April 7, 1874 | 149,543 |
| Sweeting, James A. | Device for rolling cigarettes | Nov. 30, 1897 | 594,501 |
| Sweeting, James A. | Combined knife and scoop | June 7, 1898 | 605,209 |
| Tankins, Sacramenta G. | Comb | May 11, 1920 | 1,339,632 |
| Tankins, Sacramenta G. | Method and means for treating human hair | Feb. 16, 1932 | 1,845,208 |
| Tate, Charles W. | Flexible and transparent lubricant housing for universal joint | Jan. 28, 1969 | 3,423,959 |
| Taylor, Asa J. | Machine for assembling or disassembling the parts of spring tensioned devices | June 16, 1942 | 2,286,695 |
| Taylor, Asa J. | Fluid joint | Jan. 13, 1948 | 2,434,629 |
| Taylor, Benjamin H. | Improvement in rotary engines | April 23, 1878 | 202,888 |

# Lawnie Taylor's dedicated work in the development of solar technology for use in the home became a major factor in new energy resources

Dr. Lawnie Taylor is a solar technologist and a determined scientist who is deeply involved in the research and development of solar technology. Educated at Columbia University in New York and the University of Southern California, Taylor spent many years working for the National Aeronautics and Space Administration (NASA), the Xerox Corporation, and the Nuclear Laboratory at Columbia University. Taylor received a NASA award for his development of an Apollo experiment. In 1975, Taylor joined the United States Energy Research and Development Administration. While there he began his work in the field of solar energy. One of his major areas of research included the refinement of current solar technology so it could be adapted for the home. Lawnie Taylor is a dedicated scientist committed to his community. He uses his vast scientific knowledge and creative mind to support projects such as economic development and educational advancement for the disadvantaged and the understanding of science and technology by the common person.

# AFRICAN AMERICAN INVENTORS

| Inventor | Description of Invention | Date | Patent No. |
|---|---|---|---|
| Taylor, Benjamin H. | Slide valve | July 6, 1897 | 585,798 |
| Taylor, Christopher L. | Combination toothbrush and dentifrice dispenser | Oct. 1, 1957 | 2,807,818 |
| Taylor, Moddie Daniel | Preparation of anhydrous alkaline earth halides | Aug. 6, 1957 | 2,801,899 |
| Taylor, Moddie Daniel | Ion exchange adsorption process for plutonium separation | July 11, 1961 | 2,992,249 |
| Taylor, Moddie Daniel | Preparation of anhydrous lithium salts | Aug. 14, 1962 | 3,049,406 |
| Taylor, Richard | Leaf holder | June 22, 1937 | D 105,037 |
| Thomas, Edward H. C. | Automobile key and license holder | Nov. 27, 1928 | 1,693,006 |
| Thomas, Samuel E. | Waste trap | Oct. 16, 1883 | 286,746 |
| Thomas, Samuel E. | Waste traps for basins, closets, etc. | Oct. 4, 1887 | 371,107 |
| Thomas, S. E. | Process of casting | July 31, 1888 | 386,941 |

| Inventor | Description of Invention | Date | Patent No. |
|---|---|---|---|
| Thomas, S. E. | Pipe connection | Oct. 9, 1888 | 390,821 |
| Thomas, Valerie L. | Illusion transmitter | Oct. 21, 1980 | 4,229,761 |
| Thompson, John P. | Motor vehicle elevating and parking device | July 6, 1937 | 2,086,142 |
| Thompson, Joseph Ausbon | Foot warmer | May 25, 1948 | 2,442,026 |
| Thompson, Joseph Ausbon | Moist/dry lavatory and toilet tissue | Nov. 25, 1975 | 3,921,802 |
| Thompson, Oliver L. | Vehicle parking attachment | June 9, 1925 | 1,541,670 |
| Thornton, Benjamin F. | Apparatus for automatically recording telephone messages | Nov. 10, 1931 | 1,831,331 |
| Thornton, Benjamin F. | Apparatus for automatically transmitting messages over a telephone line | Feb. 2, 1932 | 1,843,849 |
| Toland, Mary | Float-operated circuit-closer | May 4, 1920 | 1,339,239 |
| Toliver, George | Propeller for vessels | April 18, 1891 | 451,086 |

| Inventor | Description of Invention | Date | Patent No. |
|---|---|---|---|
| Toomey, Richard E.S. and Evans, James C. | Airplane appliance to prevent ice formation | March 11, 1930 | 1,749,858 |
| Turner, Allen H. | Electrostatic paint system | Jan. 16, 1962 | 3,017,115 |
| Turner, Allen H. | Electrostatic painting | Sept. 18, 1962 | 3,054,697 |
| Turner, John R. | Method and apparatus for polishing glass and like substances | July 10, 1945 | 2,380,275 |
| Turner, Madeline M. | Fruit press | April 25, 1916 | 1,180,959 |
| Vincent, Simon | Woodworking machine | Dec. 7, 1920 | 1,361,295 |
| Vincent, William and Olsen, Robert W. | Pressure relief panel hold open apparatus and method | Dec. 21, 1993 | 5,271,189 |
| Thornton, Benjamin F. | Apparatus for automatically recording telephone messages | Nov. 10, 1931 | 1,831,331 |
| Vincent, William and Olsen, Robert W. | Pressure relief panel hold open apparatus and method | May 23, 1995 | 5,417,014 |

# Art Walker launched 14 telescopes in NASA's first Multi-Spectral Solar Telescope Array flight in 1991 and 19 telescopes in the second flight

Arthur B. C. Walker, II was born in Cleveland, Ohio in 1936. He received a baccalaureate degree in physics with honors from Cleveland's Case Institute of Technology in 1957. He earned a master's degree in 1958 and a doctorate in 1962 from the University of Illinois with a dissertation on the use of radiation to produce the particles that bind protons and neutrons together in the atomic nucleus. After completing his military duty in 1965, he joined the Space Physics Laboratory of the Aerospace Corporation where for nine years he conducted pioneering physics experiment to study sun and upper atmosphere of the Earth. After arriving at Stanford, Walker directed the student observatory and taught astronomy courses including the Popular Applied Physics 15 and Physics 50 (Observational Astronomy). He became a Professor of Physics in 1974. Walker launched 14 telescopes in NASA's first Multi-Spectral Solar Telescope Array flight in 1991 and 19 telescopes in the second flight. Arrays of telescopes allow researchers to look at different temperatures throughout the sun and gain a greater understanding of solar activity. In 2000, Walker received a Distinguished Public Service Medal in recognition of four decades of distinguished scholarship, various achievements in experimental space sciences and extensive service to NASA and the nation on many advisory and review boards. Arthur B. C. Walker, II died in 2001.

# AFRICAN AMERICAN INVENTORS

| Inventor | Description of Invention | Date | Patent No. |
|---|---|---|---|
| Vincent, William and Olsen, Robert W. | Foot grilles | May 7, 1996 | 5,513,472 |
| Vincent, William and Olsen, Robert W. | Modular louver system | May 25, 1999 | 5,906,083 |
| Wade, William L. | Method of making a porous carbon cathode, a porous carbon cathode so made, and electrochemical cell including the porous carbon cathode | April 30, 1985 | 4,514,478 |
| Walker, M. Lucius, Jr. | Laminar fluid NOR element | Nov. 18, 1969 | 3,478,764 |
| Walker, Peter | Machine for cleaning seed cotton | Feb. 16, 1897 | 577,153 |
| Walker, Peter | Bait holder | March 8, 1898 | 600,241 |
| Waller, Joseph W. | Shoemaker-s cabinet or bench | Feb. 3, 1880 | 224,253 |
| Walton, Ulysses S. | Denture | March 23, 1943 | 2,314,674 |
| Warren, Richard | Display rack | March 8, 1927 | 1,619,900 |

# With the invention of the heating comb, Madame C. J. Walker became one of the most successful of all black businesswomen in the country

Hair-care entrepreneur Madame C. J. Walker was born Sarah Breedlove in Delta, Louisiana. Walker attended school at night in St. Louis, Mo., and early in her career she assisted in inventing a metal heating comb and conditioner for straightening hair. Beginning as a door-to-door peddler of her cosmetic products, she eventually amassed a fortune and Walker Beauty Products evolved into a chain of salons. In 1910, Walker built a factory in Indianapolis, Indiana to manufacture her hair preparations, facial creams, and other products. Walker became one of the foremost social leaders of her time and an African American benefactor. Marjorie Stewart Joyner invented the Permanent Waving Machine and the patent was assigned to Madame C. J. Walker's company. Walker became the first "self-made" female millionaire in the United States.

# AFRICAN AMERICAN INVENTORS

| Inventor | Description of Invention | Date | Patent No. |
|---|---|---|---|
| Washington, Wade | Corn husking machine | Aug. 14, 1883 | 283,173 |
| Watkins, Isaac | Scrubbing frame | Oct. 7, 1890 | 437,849 |
| Watts, Julius R. | Drill for boring and reaming | May 5, 1891 | 451,789 |
| Watts, Julius R. | Bracket for miners' lamps | March 7, 1893 | 493,137 |
| Weatherby, Dennis W. | Automatic dishwasher detergent composition (Cascade) | Dec. 22, 1987 | 4,714,562 |
| Weaver, Rufus J. | Stairclimbing wheelchair | Nov. 19, 1968 | 3,411,598 |
| Webb, Henry C. | Clearing plow | May 15, 1917 | 1,226,425 |
| Webster, John W. | Method and apparatus for visually comparing files in data processing system | Aug. 25, 1992 | 5,142,619 |
| Weir, Charles E. | High-pressure optical cell | Feb. 26, 1963 | 3,079,505 |
| West, Edward H. | Weather shield | Sept. 5, 1899 | 632,385 |

## James E. West became a renown inventor with the Electroacoustic Transducer Electret Microphone

James E. West was born in Prince Edward County, Virginia. While attending Temple University, he interned at Bell Labs during his summer breaks and upon his graduation in 1957, he joined the company and began work in electroacoustics, physical acoustics, and architectural acoustics. In 1962, West and Gerhard Sessler patented the electret microphone while working at Bell Laboratories. In the electret microphone, thin sheets of polymer electret film are metal coated on one side to form the membrane of the movable plate capacitor that converts sound to electrical signals with high-fidelity. The microphone became widely used because of its high performance, accuracy, and reliability in addition to its low cost, small size and lightweight. Ninety percent of today's microphones are electret microphones and they are used in everyday items such as telephones, camcorders, and tape recorders. West is the recipient of over 200 U.S. and foreign patents. He is also the leader of a program aimed at minority high school students, encouraging them to experience science with the assistance of mentors at Bell Labs.

# AFRICAN AMERICAN INVENTORS

| Inventor | Description of Invention | Date | Patent No. |
|---|---|---|---|
| West, James Edward | Technique for fabrication of foil electret | March 23, 1976 | 3,945,112 |
| West, James Edward | Technique for removing surface and volume charges from thin high polymer films | Feb. 3, 1981 | 4,248,808 |
| West, James Edward | Noise reduction processing arrangement for microphone arrays | Jan. 31, 1989 | 4,802,227 |
| West, John W. | Improvement in wagons | Oct. 18, 1870 | 108,419 |
| Wharton, Ferdinand D. | Treatment of diarrhea employing certain basic polyelectrolyte polymers | April 11, 1972 | 3,655,869 |
| White, Charles Fred | Timing device | Feb. 27, 1912 | 1,018,799 |
| White, Daniel L. | Extension step for cars | Jan. 12, 1897 | 574,969 |
| White, John T. | Lemon squeezer | Dec. 8, 1896 | 572,849 |
| Wicks, Jerome L. | Patio door and window guard system invention | April 20, 1982 | 4,325,203 |

| Inventor | Description of Invention | Date | Patent No. |
|---|---|---|---|
| Wiles, Joseph S. | Injection pistol | Nov. 10, 1970 | 3,538,916 |
| Williams, Carter | Canopy frame | Feb. 2, 1892 | 468,280 |
| Williams, James P. | Pillow sham holder | Oct. 10, 1899 | 634,784 |
| Williams, Paul E. | Helicopter | Nov. 27, 1962 | 3,065,933 |
| Williams, Philip B. | Electrically controlled and operated railway switch | Jan. 15, 1901 | 666,080 |
| Williams, Robert M. | Method and apparatus for disinfecting | Dec. 15, 1992 | 5,171,523 |
| Wilson, Donald C. | Flying saucer toy | Oct. 21, 1980 | 4,228,616 |
| Winn, Frank | Direct acting steam engine | Dec. 4, 1888 | 394,047 |
| Winters, Joseph R. | Fire escape ladder | May 7, 1878 | 203,517 |
| Winters, Joseph R. | Improvement in fire escape ladder | April 8, 1879 | 214,224 |

# In 1891, Dr. Daniel Hale Williams founded Provident Hospital in Chicago where he later performed the first successful open heart surgery in 1893

Daniel Hale Williams was born in Hollidaysburg, Pennsylvania in 1856. He operated a barbershop in Wisconsin in 1873 before apprenticing himself to Dr. Henry Palmer, the Surgeon General of Wisconsin in 1878. When Williams graduated from medical school, his teachers and colleagues knew he had a brilliant career ahead. He soon established a booming private practice and held a position as surgeon and instructor of anatomy at Chicago Medical College. Because he was black he was not allowed to use the medical facilities at any of the hospitals in the area. In 1890, Williams launched a drive to found a biracial hospital. As a result of his efforts, Provident Hospital in Chicago, IL was incorporated in 1891. This was the first hospital in the nation founded and controlled by African Americans. It was at Provident Hospital in 1893 that Dr. Williams performed his famous open-heart operation, the first operation of its kind done successfully. On July 9, 1893, he saved the life of a knifing victim by sewing up his heart. Williams was appointed by President Grover Cleveland as Surgeon-in-Chief of Freedman's Hospital in Washington, D.C. in 1893. Dr. Williams was the first black to become a Fellow of the American College of Surgeons in 1913.

# O.S. (Ozzie) Williams helped to develop the first airborne radar system to locate crashed planes

O.S. (Ozzie) Williams was born in 1921. He became an aeronautical engineer through persistent hard work. During World War II, he helped develop the first airborne radar system that was helpful in locating planes that had crashed. After the war and during the sixties, he became part of a handful of African American technical staff in the aerospace industry when he went to work at the Grumman Corporation. Under a Grumman contract with NASA, Williams supervised the development of the small rocket engines that helped save the lives of the astronauts aboard Apollo 13 in April 1970. Williams became a vice president at Grumman. He later, became part of a program to harness wind and solar energy and supply the African continent with the energy it needs. O.S. Williams is a scientist committed to improving the future for all of mankind and providing role models for all future generations.

## AFRICAN AMERICAN INVENTORS

| Inventor | Description of Invention | Date | Patent No. |
|---|---|---|---|
| Wood, Francis J. | Potato digger | April 23, 1895 | 537,953 |
| Woodard, Dudley G. | Preparation of water soluble acrylic copolymers for use in water treatment | April 6, 1971 | 3,574,175 |
| Woods, Granville T. | Steam boiler furnace | June 3, 1884 | 299,894 |
| Woods, Granville T. | Telephone transmitter | Dec. 2, 1884 | 308,817 |
| Woods, Granville T. | Apparatus for transmissions of messages by electricity | April 7, 1885 | 315,368 |
| Woods, Granville T. | Relay instrument | June 7, 1887 | 364,619 |
| Woods, Granville T. | Polarized relay | July 5, 1887 | 366,192 |
| Woods, Granville T. | Electromechanical brake | Aug. 16, 1887 | 368,265 |
| Woods, Granville T. | Telephone system and apparatus | Oct. 11, 1887 | 371,241 |

# Granville T. Woods was one of the most prolific American inventors in history. He revolutionized the transportation and communications industries worldwide and was hailed by fellow inventors as "The Black Edison"

Granville T. Woods was born in Columbus, Ohio in 1856. He was one of the greatest inventors in the country who revolutionized transportation and communications throughout the world. Just before the turn of the century, trolley cars and trains were the main means of transportation but they were also extremely dangerous. Woods helped alleviate much of the danger when he invented the telephone transmitter, which was bought by Bell Telephone Company in 1885. Later, Woods invented an overhead wire power system for trolley and freight cars and a "third rail" system to keep cars running on the proper tracks. Railroads are particularly indebted to this African American inventor for his development of a new air brake and a system that enabled moving trains to send telegraph messages to each other which prevented many accidents. The Edison and Phelps companies who claimed priority for Thomas Edison challenged Woods in federal court, but Woods eventually won the patent rights. Woods also sold many of his electrical inventions to General Electric, Westinghouse and to Bell Telephone Company. Among his other top inventions are the steam boiler furnace, the incubator and the roller coaster, for a total of 50 patents. Granville T. Woods died in 1910.

## AFRICAN AMERICAN INVENTORS

| Inventor | Description of Invention | Date | Patent No. |
|---|---|---|---|
| Woods, Granville T. | Electromagnetic brake apparatus | Oct. 18, 1887 | 371,655 |
| Woods, Granville T. | Railway telegraphy | Nov. 15, 1887 | 373,383 |
| Woods, Granville T. | Induction telegraph system | Nov. 29, 1887 | 373,915 |
| Woods, Granville T. | Overhead conducting system for electric railways | May 29, 1888 | 383,844 |
| Woods, Granville T. | Electromotive railway | June 26, 1888 | 385,034 |
| Woods, Granville T. | Tunnel construction for electric railways | July 17, 1988 | 386,282 |
| Woods, Granville T. | Galvanic battery | Aug. 14, 1888 | 387,839 |
| Woods, Granville T. | Railway telegraphy | Aug. 28, 1888 | 388,803 |
| Woods, Granville T. | Automatic safety cut-out for electric circuits | Jan. 1, 1889 | 395,533 |
| Woods, Granville T. | Automatic safety cut-out for electric circuits | Oct. 14, 1890 | 438,590 |

| Inventor | Description of Invention | Date | Patent No. |
|---|---|---|---|
| Woods, Granville T. | Electric railway system | Nov. 10, 1891 | 463,020 |
| Woods, Granville T. | Electric railway supply system | Oct. 31, 1893 | 507,606 |
| Woods, Granville T. | Electric railway conduit | Nov. 21, 1893 | 509,065 |
| Woods, Granville T. | System of electrical distribution | Oct. 13, 1896 | 569,443 |
| Woods, Granville T. | System of electrical distribution | Aug. 1, 1899 | 630,280 |
| Woods, Granville T. | Amusement apparatus (Roller Coaster) | Dec. 19, 1899 | 639,692 |
| Woods, Granville T. | Incubator | Aug. 28, 1900 | 656,760 |
| Woods, Granville T. | Automatic circuit-breaking apparatus | Nov. 20, 1900 | 662,049 |
| Woods, Granville T. | Electric railway | Jan. 29, 1901 | 667,110 |
| Woods, Granville T. | Electric railway system | July 9, 1901 | 678,086 |

| Inventor | Description of Invention | Date | Patent No. |
|---|---|---|---|
| Woods, Granville T. | Regulating and controlling electrical translating devices | Sept. 3, 1901 | 681,768 |
| Woods, Granville T. | Electric railway | Nov. 19, 1901 | 687,098 |
| Woods, Granville T. | Method of controlling electric motors or other electrical translating devices | Jan. 7, 1902 | 690,807 |
| Woods, Granville T. | Method of controlling electric motors or other electrical translating devices | Jan. 7, 1902 | 690,808 |
| Woods, Granville T. | Apparatus for controlling electric motors or other electrical translating devices | Jan. 7, 1902 | 690,809 |
| Woods, Granville T. | Apparatus for controlling electric motors or other electrical translating devices | Jan. 7, 1902 | 690,810 |
| Woods, Granville T. | Electric railway | March 25, 1902 | 695,988 |

| Inventor | Description of Invention | Date | Patent No. |
|---|---|---|---|
| Woods, Granville T. | System of electric control | April 15, 1902 | 697,767 |
| Woods, Granville T. | Motor controlling apparatus | April 15, 1902 | 697,928 |
| Woods, Granville T. | Automatic air brake | June 10, 1902 | 701,981 |
| Woods, Granville T. | Electric railway system | Jan. 13, 1903 | 718,183 |
| Woods, Granville T. and Woods, Lyates | Electric railway | May 26, 1903 | 729,481 |
| Woods, Granville T. and Woods, Lyates | Railway- brake apparatus | March 29, 1904 | 755,825 |
| Woods, Granville T. | Electric-railway apparatus | June 14, 1904 | 762,792 |
| Woods, Granville T. and Woods, Lyates | Railway-brake apparatus | July 18, 1905 | 795,243 |
| Woods, Granville T. | Vehicle-controlling apparatus | Sept. 24, 1907 | 867,180 |
| Wormley, James | Lifesaving apparatus | May 24, 1881 | 242,091 |
| Young, James E. | Battery performance control | Jan. 14, 1986 | 4,564,798 |

# The Legacy Of African Americans

The African American race has proven to be one of the strongest, most intellectual, and durable races in the history of mankind. To have suffered the most extensive holocaust of a single race in which approximately tens of millions of lives were lost during the dreadful Middle Passage and African slave trade that lasted over 400 years; to endure the government sanctioned discrimination that kept them in the throes of poverty; to have faced the murderous nightriders in the form of the hate spewing Ku Klux Klan who burned crosses, homes, schools, churches, and conducted public lynching of blacks; to have faced all of this horrible and awesome adversity and still manage to reach the pinnacle in various professions displays a physical and mental strength, and intellectual capacity never before exhibited by any single race of humans.

Despite all of this, not only does the African American dominate many professional sports, but they have reached the top in music, entertainment, military, science, medicine, education, law, and any field of endeavor they have chosen.

Today, most African Americans recognize the disproportionate amount of black men in prisons and understand that it is not because of some mythical inherent criminal tendency, but it is because of a pattern and practice of systematic racial discrimination aimed primarily at black men in employment and in our court systems. This discrimination in our court systems runs concurrent with the racial discrimination in our national employment levels. Over 73 percent of the people who commit crimes are unemployed at the times the crimes are committed. As a result, all of this black brainpower, capabilities and muscle sit behind bars, untapped, while our nation's infrastructure crumbles from lack of maintenance. These black men want to work and support their families to keep them together, but they get jail instead of jobs, and every citizen is paying the price. This country has more people in jail today than any other industrial country in the world.

In August 2002 the Justice Policy Institute, an advocacy group based in Washington reported, that in 2000, 791,600 black men were in jail or prison and 603,032 were enrolled in colleges or universities. By contrast, the study said that in 1980, 143,000 African American men were in jail or prison while 463,700 were enrolled in colleges or universities. Some criminal-justice experts cautioned that the comparison was misleading because the number in jail and prison included all adult black men ranging upwards from 17 years old, while the number in institutions of higher learning was in a much smaller age range.

It is vital that all African Americans realize their individual potential and compare their lives and goals with those of their ancestors. Today, no matter what one's choice of field may be, we should recognize that it will be much easier to pursue any goal because of those who went before us. These trailblazers faced the hate, bigotry, poverty, and discouragement from a world that was ignorant of the African American's intellectual and physical ability. Past historians completely and purposely obliterated black history from school textbooks in order to discourage future blacks from ambitious aspirations to achieve, and still many African Americans prevailed. It is a mandatory prerequisite that all blacks feel proud of their heritage and realize that our African American ancestry is our badge of courage for the truth will set you free.

Many black children grow up unable to identify with suitable black role models because as far as they know, there are none. This is grossly untrue because as this book has clearly shown, there are plenty of African American role models in all walks of life. However, the American media has tried to maintain the myth of black inferiority. The lack of blacks in dramatic roles in the television and motion picture industry and the lack of African American dramatic continuing family TV series reinforces the misconception that blacks are not to be taken seriously.

Consequently, it is essential that each and every American, black and white, should recognize the legacy of our African American ancestors and value this legacy that has, and continues to this day, to enhance the lives of all mankind. The insidious act of completely hiding the history of an entire race of people to sustain a false premise built upon distortions, omissions, exaggerations, and blatant lies is one of the most denigrating and awesome forms of racial discrimination ever perpetrated.

The Million Man March in October 1995 signaled a new era of black responsibility and the black men in attendance were determined to end their frustration from poverty and racism. They do not want any handouts or welfare. All they want is an equal opportunity to gain a better quality of life for themselves and their families. All of the drastic effects of unemployment and disenfranchisement have demonstrated a clear relationship between economic downturns and increases in admissions to mental hospitals. No major factor other than economic instability appears to influence variation in mental hospital rates. These findings also include cardiovascular disease, infant mortality, child abuse, spouse abuse, and suicide. Recent studies have verified a condition of high blood pressure by victims of systematic racial discrimination. It is therefore, imperative, that African Americans be given a fair and equal opportunity to attain a better quality of life by utilizing their maximum capabilities to obtain employment.

All of these previous and current inventions, innovations and accomplishments listed in this book clearly show how important it is to get this information to the younger generations who are constantly being barraged by negative stereotypes on television, in motion pictures and in the press. For some strange reason the people who own the publishing businesses do not want the truth about African Americans to come out. What are they afraid of?

The people who teach our kids have never been properly educated about the contributions of African Americans and the white people who are aware of these many accomplishments are reluctant to pass on this knowledge for fear of retaliation or ridicule from other whites.

In our society, we are still being taught that the contributions of most African Americans are in sports, entertainment and the arts. However, scientific innovations and inventions developed by African Americans have saved and changed many lives. Recognition of accomplishments by African American scientists provides role models and unlimited inspiration for young people and refutes claims of intellectual inferiority of the race. It is important to counter the academic nonsense of *The Bell Curve* and the long, untrue history of *white supremacy* propagandized by carefully altered and distorted facts. How does the person that created the *Bell Curve* explain the more than 1100 African American inventions and the physicians, scientists and engineers in this book? When we discuss black inventors we clearly show that racial inferiority is not the case. These are bright, intelligent people. In fact, the African American race has contributed more to world civilization than any other minority segment of the American population.

The anti-affirmative action policies in Texas and California have forced African Americans to take a step backwards in trying to obtain an equal opportunity in education. In some law and medical schools in those states there has been a decline of as much as 81 percent in black enrollment. This anti-affirmative action has come about because many Americans are accepting the argument that educational opportunities must be given out solely on the basis of standardized tests, or academic grades, and that college admissions officers may not factor in judgements in human potential, previous disadvantages, character, or the benefits of racially and culturally diverse student bodies. Maybe this anti-affirmative action policy indicates that it is time for African Americans to retaliate by turning down sports scholarships to the schools in those states until this racist policy is discontinued. This would certainly effect these colleges in their turnstile profits from major sports events when their sports program decline from the inability to field a competitive team in football, basketball, and baseball. As a result, many white star athletes would also turn down scholarships to those schools because they would not want to be associated with any school with a losing sports program since it could affect their future opportunities for a professional career and contractual negotiations. How would these schools compete with major colleges back east if they had no African American players?

The true meaning of an educational opportunity cannot be over emphasized and it is important to keep it in the proper perspective. As an example, twelve years ago, Shantwania Buchanan was sitting in a juvenile lockup in Mississippi, just another poor black girl whose life seemed prescribed by poverty, a crack-addicted mother, homelessness and crime. Always an excellent student, through the opportunity given to her by a $20,000 Coca Cola Scholarship and the confidence of former Mississippi governor William Winter, she graduated from Brown University in May 2001 and emerged as Dr. Shantwania Buchanan. In June, she began a medical residency as an obstetrician-gynecologist candidate at Northwestern University Medical Center.

It is important for all to remember that the remains of the skeleton discovered in Africa and reported by the National Geographic Society, were more than three and a half million years old and it confirmed the fact that the origin of man was in Africa. Four distinct routes leading from Africa to Europe and Asia indicate that the continent of Africa is where these different races originated. So when we speak of African ancestry are we not speaking of the ancestors of man? . Is it a mere coincident that four fifths of the world's population is of the darker races?

In conclusion, it is important that the accomplishments of the African Americans outlined in this book be made available to all Americans as we come together in the 21st century. This information will stimulate the intellectual growth in all of our lives, bring people closer together, and encourage a better understanding and respect between the races as we encourage each individual to strive for maximum success to accomplish their goals. If those African Americans were able to achieve success in spite of the insurmountable obstacles and adversities they faced when America was struggling to survive, today we should be able to accomplish our goals and full potential much easier in an environment that is more conducive to success in achieving our goals for every man, woman, and child. Much of this has been made possible because of the legacy of our African American ancestors who thrived by their creativity and foresight. So, if you're ever asked that familiar question, *"What has the African American ever contributed to this country?"* You will be well versed and prepared to answer at length.

# Index

# B

# C

# D

# E

# H

# M

# N

Russell, Joseph L., 160
Russell, Lewis A., 160
Ryder, Earl, 160

# S

Sadgwar, Daniel A. 149
Safety attachment for automotive
 vehicles, 124
Safety gate for bridges, 151
Safety system for operating railroads, 58
Safety window cleaning device, 161
Sammons, Walter H., 160
Samms, Adolphus, 160
Sampson, George T., 161
Sampson, Henry Thomas, 161
Sand band for wagon, 23
Sanderson, Dewey S.C., 161
Sanderson, Ralph W., 161
Sanitarium, 59
Sanitary attachment for drinking
 glasses, 137
Sanitary belt, 119
Satcher, Dr. David, 159
Saxton, Richard L., 161
Schaal, Arkansas, 72
Scharschmidt, Virginia, 161
Scholar, 53
Science fields, 88
Scientific American, 15
Scott, Henry, 162
Scott, Howard L., 162
Scott, J. C., 162
Scott, Linzy, 162
Scott, Robert P., 162
Scottron, Samuel R., 162
Scrubbing Frame, 179
Sealing attachment for bottles, 94
Seasoning material derived form red
 peppers, 87
Secretary of Interior, 11
Secure cryptographic logic arrangement,
42
Seed planter, 32
Segregated hospital, 61
Self propelled toy fish, 124
Self supporting electrical resistor
composed
 of glass, 35
Self-binding harvester, 65

Self-directing headlight, 138
Self-feeding attachment for furnaces, 37
Self-leveling table, 18
Self-setting animal trap, 42
Self-starting gasoline engine, 112
Semicond. Devices/Optical transitions, 21
Sensitizing photographic media, 128
Separating fluids with selective
 membranes, 168
Separating screen, 68
Separation of distillable isocyanates, 49
Server for automatic serving systems, 66
Service apparatus for dining rooms, 66
Sessler, Gerhard, 180
Shadow box, 162
Shampoo head rest, 21
Shaw, Earl D., 163
Shock falsing inhibitor circuit, 70
Shoe industry, 131
Shoe lasting machine, 131
Shoe machinery trade, 131
Shoe sole with an adjustable support
 pattern, 62
Shoe, 60
Shoemaker's cabinet or bench, 177
Shoemaker's jack, 49
Shorter, Dennis W., 163
Shower bath spray, 143
Shower wall and bath tub mounted back
 washer, 119
Shutter and fastening, 49
Shutter worker, 149
Siamese twins, 43
Signal apparatus high water indicator for
 bridges, 21
Signal generator, 38
Signal generators, 19
Signaling device, 52
Sigur, Wanda A., 163
Silvera, Esteban, 163
Simpson College, 45
Skanks, Stephen Chambers, 163
Sled propeller, 161
Sleeping car berth register, 163
Slide valve, 173
Small, Isadore, 163
Smartt, Brinay, 163
Smith, Bernard , 164
Smith, John Winsor, 164
Smith, Johnathan S., 164
Smith, Joseph H., 164
Smith, Mildred E., 164
Smith, Morris L., 164
Smith, Peter D., 166
Smith, Robert T., 166
Smith, Samuel C., 166

Printed in the United States
1130100001B/94-148